Roussel Davids Byles

**The second epistle of Saint Paul to the Corinthians**

Roussel Davids Byles

**The second epistle of Saint Paul to the Corinthians**

ISBN/EAN: 9783337336295

Printed in Europe, USA, Canada, Australia, Japan

Cover: Foto ©Lupo / pixelio.de

More available books at **www.hansebooks.com**

ST. EDMUND'S COLLEGE SERIES OF SCRIPTURE HANDBOOKS.

# THE SECOND EPISTLE
## OF SAINT PAUL
# TO THE CORINTHIANS

WITH INTRODUCTION AND NOTES

BY

R. D. BYLES, B.A.

LATE SCHOLAR OF BALLIOL COLLEGE, OXFORD

LONDON
CATHOLIC TRUTH SOCIETY
69 SOUTHWARK BRIDGE ROAD, S.E.;
245 BROMPTON ROAD, S.W.; 22 PATERNOSTER ROW.
1897

**Nihil Obstat**
   Johannes McIntyre, D.D.
       *Censor Deputatus*


**Imprimatur**
   Herbertus Cardinalis Vaughan
       *Archiepiscopus Westmonasteriensis*

# PREFACE.

THE present volume is intended to assist any who wish for help in understanding the argument and the circumstances of the Epistle of which it treats, as well as to serve as a text-book for the use of students.

The text is that of Burns and Oates' sixpenny Testament; with the exception of two obvious misprints, and a few cases of punctuation.

My special thanks are due to the Right Rev. Mgr. Ward for his assistance during the progress of the work; and to the Rev. Dr. McIntyre, who in reading through the proof sheets, has very kindly furnished many valuable suggestions.

R. D. BYLES.

St. Edmund's College
  November, 1897.

# CONTENTS.

INTRODUCTION—

    Chapter I. St. Paul . . . . . . . ix

    Chapter II. The Companions of St. Paul mentioned in this Epistle . . . . . . . xv

    Chapter III. The Church of Corinth . . . . xviii

    Chapter IV. The Second Epistle to the Corinthians    xxii

    Chapter V. The Text of this Epistle . xxiii

TEXT AND NOTES . . . 1–85

APPENDIX—

    I. Visits of St. Paul to Corinth .    86

    II. The Ecstasy of St. Paul .    87

    III. The " Sting of the Flesh " . . 88

    IV. The " Letter " and the " Spirit " . . 90

# INTRODUCTION.

## CHAPTER I.

### ST. PAUL.

THE events of St. Paul's public life are narrated in the Acts of the Apostles as far as they are known; so that it is not necessary in this place to give more than a short account of them, collecting the scattered references which might escape notice, and referring to the Scripture text for the longer narrative. But concerning his earlier life, and also about his last years, a rather fuller account is required. St. Paul was a Jew, of the tribe of Benjamin, born, not in Palestine, but at Tarsus, a city of Cilicia, the natives of which enjoyed the privileges of Roman citizenship (cf. Acts xvi. 37, 38, xxi. 39, xxii. 3, 25–29). He received at his circumcision the name of Saul. He was brought up in the sect of the Pharisees, which sect, though it contained many hypocrites, included also most of the really fervent and pious men among the Jews. In accordance with the precept of the Jewish law, that every young man must learn some trade by which he could support himself, Saul was instructed in the art of tent-making. For his higher education he was sent at an early age to Jerusalem, where he became a pupil of the Rabbi Gamaliel, one of the most famous men among the Jews of his time both for piety and learning. Under his care Saul received a thorough education in the truths and precepts of the Jewish law, and became known as a fervent and zealous Pharisee (Acts xxii. 3, xxiii. 6, xxvi. 4-7; Phil. iii. 5-7). The education which he received at this time as a Pharisee was the source to him of both good and harm. On the one hand, he became thoroughly acquainted with the facts of revelation, so far as they were known to the Jews; his faith in the resurrection and in other supernatural facts was strengthened; and his acquaintance with the prophecies led him to expect the coming of the promised Messiah. By these means the way was prepared for his ultimate conversion. On the other hand, though there is no reason to believe that St. Paul was guilty of the hypocrisy and ostentation of religion which our Lord frequently rebuked in the Pharisees, yet it appears that his training in this sect, the national pride of which led it to reject a religion which offered to embrace publicans and heathen, and to give his just rights even to a Roman conqueror, was responsible for the fury with which at first he persecuted the Church of God (cf. Gal. i. 13, 14). Saul was still a young man when the newly-founded Christian Church first began to be known in Jerusalem. His early training had filled him with a zeal for the law, and he had not learned that tolerance of what is not known to be evil which characterized his great master, Gamaliel (cf. Acts v. 34-39). Consequently he became one of the most violent persecutors of the Church. He occupied a prominent position at the martyrdom of St. Stephen (Acts vii. 57-59); and committed to prison very many Christians (Acts viii. 3; cf. xxii. 4, 5, xxvi. 9-11). Not content with this, but being anxious to entirely root out the infant Church, he obtained letters from the Jewish Sanhedrin to the synagogues of Damascus, empowering him to seize and bring to Jerusalem any Christians found in that city.

Up to this time he never seems to have suspected the possible truth of the Christian Faith (cf. Acts xxvi. 9). Though a persecutor, he was in good faith. The prejudices of his early training were so great that nothing short of a miracle seemed capable of removing them. But as he came near to Damascus, at midday, a great light suddenly shone round him, and our Lord Himself revealed to him the truth of that religion which he had been vainly endeavouring to suppress. His correspondence with this miraculous grace was perfect (Acts xxvi. 19). He rose from the ground blind, but already prepared to accept the Christian Faith. After three days, which he spent in prayer, a Christian dwelling in Damascus, named Ananias, came to him in obedience to another vision, and restored his sight and gave him baptism.

After this miraculous conversion St. Paul remained a short time at Damascus, proving to the Jews in that city that Jesus was the Messiah. But the time appointed by God for him to commence his missionary labours had not yet arrived. A long period of preparation was first necessary.

Accordingly he retired from Damascus into the wilderness of Arabia, where he lived for some time a solitary life. On his return to Damascus a plot was formed by the Jews to take his life when he passed through the city gates (Acts ix. 23, 24): and therefore, when he went to Jerusalem, he was obliged to escape by night, being let down in a basket over the wall (Acts ix. 25 ; 2 Cor. xi. 33). The object of this visit to Jerusalem (which took place three years after his conversion) was to see the prince of the apostles (Gal. i. 18), to whom it was plainly desirable that his conversion should be made known before he began his apostolic labours. He stayed at Jerusalem fifteen days : but as another plot was formed against his life, the Christians sent him away to his native city of Tarsus, where he remained in retirement for four years more (Gal. i. 18, 19 ; Acts ix. 26–30). At the end of this time he was brought by his friend Barnabas to Antioch (Acts xi. 25), and soon afterwards these two went to Jerusalem with contributions for the relief of the poor in that city. It was after his return from this mission, some seven or eight years after his conversion, that a direct inspiration of the Holy Ghost ordered him to be ordained, together with St. Barnabas, for the purpose of missionary work, especially amongst the Gentiles (Acts xiii. 2, 3).

It is not necessary to follow in detail the events of St. Paul's life during his missionary labours which followed this ordination.  His first journey took him in company with St. Barnabas through Cyprus and a large part of Asia Minor, where they made a great number of converts (cf. Acts xiii., xiv.).  It was about this time also that the apostle seems to have changed his name from Saul to Paul (Acts xiii. 9).  On returning from this journey he stayed for some years at Antioch, until a dispute which arose about the obligation of circumcision for Gentile converts caused him to go to Jerusalem to attend the Council held in that city to settle this difficulty (Acts xv.).  After the Council he returned to Antioch, and continued there some time longer before setting out on his second missionary journey.  In this journey he was accompanied by St. Silas, and, after passing through Asia Minor, he received a direct inspiration ordering him to cross over into Europe.  Accordingly he traversed Macedonia and Achaia, founding churches in those cities which he visited; and after a stay of eighteen months at Corinth, he returned to Jerusalem and to Antioch (Acts xvi.–xviii).  His stay at Antioch on this occasion seems to have been very short, and he soon commenced a third journey, in the course of which he remained more than two years at Ephesus, and then, after visiting Corinth, returned to Jerusalem (Acts xviii. 23–xxi. 16). On arriving here he found that a number of the Christian Jews, who were much devoted to the Jewish law, were very liable to be scandalized at any teaching in opposition to it. They supposed that their conversion to Christianity did not release them from the ceremonial obligations imposed upon them by their birth as Jews.  St. Paul's own practice had always been to teach that these ceremonies were no longer of obligation, but at the same time it appears that he himself conformed to them, to avoid giving any scandal.

Nevertheless, his teaching had been misrepresented by some, who said that in his preaching he had told the Jews who lived amongst the Gentiles that it was positively wrong for them to follow the law to which they had been accustomed.  In order to show how false this charge was, he went to the Temple, at the request of some of the Jerusalem Christians, to purify himself openly, accompanied by some other Jewish Christians, who were completing the term of their vows. Nevertheless this act, undertaken to satisfy the Jewish Christians, proved to be the occasion of his ruin at the hands of the unconverted Jews, who, seeing him in the Temple, supposed that he had brought some of his Gentile companions into that building, and therefore stirred up a riot against him. The result was that the Roman tribune took him into custody, and he remained in prison at Jerusalem, at Cæsarea, and at Rome for more than five years (Acts xxii.–xxviii.). At the end of this time, probably about the year 63 A.D., he was again set at liberty.

The events of the ensuing years are involved in some obscurity. The tradition which asserts that he then made his intended visit to Spain (cf. Rom. xv. 28) is supported by the words of St. Clement, who says, writing from Rome, that St. Paul went to the utmost limits of the West. Before his release he had sent Timothy to Philippi (Phil. ii. 19–23); and in his Epistles he had expressed a hope of visiting both Philippi and Colossa (Phil. ii. 24; and Philemon i. 22). It appears that he went to Macedonia (1 Tim. i. 3), probably after visiting Ephesus, and establishing St. Timothy as bishop of that city. It is also evident (Titus i. 5) that he went to Crete with St. Titus, and left him as bishop of that island, returning himself to Macedonia, and passing the ensuing winter at Nicopolis (Titus iii. 12). It seems that he also visited Corinth, Troas, and Miletus (2 Tim. iv. 13, 20). The occasion and place of his second arrest are alike unknown. It may be that it took place in the course of his travels, and that he was sent to Rome for trial; or he may have returned voluntarily to the imperial and papal city, and there have been cast into prison. During this last imprisonment he wrote his Second Epistle to St. Timothy, bidding him come to him before the ensuing winter. During part of his imprisonment he had several Christians attending on him, but at the time of writing St. Luke alone remained with him (2 Tim. iv. 9–11). At length he was condemned to death and led out to execution. As a Roman citizen he had the privilege of suffering death by beheading. The traditional scene of his martyrdom is the Three Fountains outside the gates of Rome, where a church has been erected in his honour, in which a portion of his body is preserved. His martyrdom took place under the emperor Nero, about the year A.D. 67, when he was probably a little less than sixty years of age.

There are several accounts of St. Paul's personal appearance, which agree with one another in the most important points. The earliest of these is found in the *Acts of Paul and Thecla*, an apocryphal work which is supposed by many scholars to have been composed, partially at least, in the second century, and to contain many elements of true history. In this it is said that he was *of a low stature; bald on the head; with crooked but handsome legs; with meeting eyebrows; hook-nosed; full of grace; for sometimes he appeared as a man, sometimes he had the countenance of an angel.* To this description (which does not seem like the mere product of imagination) other early writers add that he had a *stoop in his shoulders, grey eyes*, and *an ample beard*. The same description is supported by the earliest pictures which exist of the apostle, and is thoroughly in accordance with that in 2 Cor. x. 1, 10.

A fuller account of St. Paul's life and character is to be found in Butler's *Lives of the Saints* (see January 25th and June 30th). But no better knowledge of his personality can be desired than is to be obtained from a careful reading of his Epistles, in which we see portrayed his character and his work during the last fifteen years of his life. And among all his Epistles there is none in which his individuality is more strongly marked than it is in the Second Epistle to the Corinthians.

It is well known that the Protestant Reformers of the sixteenth century attempted to gain authority for their heresies by the use of isolated quotations from the writings of St. Paul; and even to-day there are some of those who are not unprepared to listen to Catholic claims, who yet think that they find in St. Paul a tone and character out of harmony with the Catholic spirit, and approximating more to Protestantism. One who was very far from understanding the Catholic religion, but who yet tried to do justice to the character of St. Paul, the late Professor Jowett, has succeeded, at least in part, in realizing how far the spirit of St. Paul was from that of the Protestant Reformers. He says: "The saints of the Middle Ages are in many respects unlike St. Paul, and yet many of them bear a far closer resemblance to him than is to be found in Luther and the Reformers. The points of resemblance which we seem to see in them, are the same withdrawal from the things of earth, the same ecstasy, the same consciousness of the person of Christ. Who would describe Luther by the words 'crucified with Christ'? It is in another manner that the Reformer was called upon to war, with weapons earthly as well as spiritual."[1] These points of resemblance which Professor Jowett notices between St. Paul and later Catholic saints are just those which cut him off entirely from the heroes of Protestantism. He may differ from some of the Saints in many things—for there are *diversities of graces* in the true Church, and there is *liberty where the Spirit of God is*—but all the Saints are alike in their detachment from the things of earth, and in their following of and real union with our Lord.

## CHAPTER II.

#### THE COMPANIONS OF ST. PAUL MENTIONED IN THIS EPISTLE

ST. TIMOTHY was a native of Lystra in Lycaonia (Acts xvi. 1). His father was a Gentile, but his mother, Eunice, a Jewess, and, like his grandmother, Lois, a Christian convert (2 Tim. i. 5). When St. Paul visited that district, receiving from the faithful there a "good testimony" of his character, he took Timothy with him to help in his labours (Acts xvi. 3). As he was in part a Jew, but had not been circumcised, St. Paul circumcised him, so as not to offend any Jewish Christians, many of whom still regarded

---

[1] St. Paul's Epistles to the Thessalonians, Galatians, and Romans, vol. i. p. 361.

this rite as binding upon Jews. He passed with St. Paul and Silas through Asia Minor and Macedonia, but remained with Silas in Berea when St. Paul was compelled to quit that city (Acts xvii. 14, 15). Not long afterwards he and Silas, being sent for by St. Paul, rejoined him at Corinth (Acts xviii. 5), where they were united to the apostle in preaching the Gospel (2 Cor. i. 19). His name is joined with that of St. Paul and Silas in the salutations at the head of both Epistles to the Thessalonians, which were written from Corinth at this time. He was with St. Paul again at Ephesus three or four years later (Acts xix. 22), but it is not certain whether he had accompanied him in the meantime. When St. Paul was intending to proceed from Ephesus into Macedonia and Achaia he sent Timothy before him with Erastus to prepare for his coming (Acts xix. 22, and 1 Cor. xvi. 10). It appears that St. Paul waited at Ephesus until his return (1 Cor. xvi. 11). They then journeyed together by way of Troas to Macedonia, where they met Titus, and where St. Paul wrote this Second Epistle to the Corinthians, in which the name of Timothy is coupled with his own (i. 1). He also accompanied St. Paul on his journey to and from Corinth (Acts. xx. 4, 5), and went before him to Troas. It is probable that he also accompanied the apostle to Jerusalem, but nothing certain is known about him until after St. Paul's arrival in Rome three years later, when St. Timothy is again mentioned in the salutations at the head of the Epistles to the Colossians, to Philemon, and to the Philippians (c. A.D. 63). Either at or about this time St. Timothy suffered imprisonment (probably at Rome), but he was released soon afterwards (Heb. xiii. 23). The history of his later life is not so fully known. Apparently he accompanied St. Paul to Ephesus, as soon as they were both set free. It is certain that he was ordained by St. Paul bishop of Ephesus, and he was apparently also Metropolitan of the Province of Asia. St. Paul wrote two letters to him—one from Macedonia, soon after his consecration, and the other from Rome while the apostle was in prison there for the second time, and was expecting his death (cf. 2 Tim. iv. 6). In this letter he begs St. Timothy to come to him before his death (2 Tim. i. 4, iv. 21). The only place in the New Testament which seems to refer to the later life of St. Timothy is in the Apocalypse (ii. 1-6), which was written by St. John probably two or three years after the date of St. Paul's Second Epistle to Timothy. In this passage the Bishop of Ephesus, although praised for many things, is yet blamed for having left his first charity and is threatened with deprivation if he does not do penance, and return to his first works. Most commentators consider that this must refer to St. Timothy, who had lost some of his early fervour. Tradition relates that he was martyred in the year 97 whilst endeavouring to oppose a heathen ceremony. His festival is observed on the 24th of January.

St. Titus was a Gentile, converted by St. Paul, whom he accompanied to the Council of Jerusalem (A.D. 51). Here some of the Judaizing teachers wished him to be circumcised, but as he was a Gentile, St. Paul would not permit it, lest he should give countenance to the contention that this rite was binding on all Christian converts (cf. Gal. ii. 1-5). During St. Paul's second missionary journey, which was commenced immediately after this Council, nothing is heard of Titus; but on the third journey he was with St. Paul at Ephesus, and was sent thence by him to Corinth, (probably immediately after the return of St. Timothy,) to heal the scandals and dissensions in that Church. He rejoined St. Paul in Macedonia when the apostle was himself on his way to Corinth (2 Cor. vii. 6; cf. ii. 13, vii. 13-15). As soon as St. Paul had heard the news he brought of the Corinthian Church, he dispatched him again to Corinth as the bearer of his Second Epistle (ibid. viii. 6, 17, 23); and followed himself soon afterwards. Nothing more is known of St. Titus until after St. Paul's first imprisonment, when he visited Crete in company with the apostle, and was left behind as bishop of that island ('Titus i. 5). In the Epistle which St. Paul wrote to him a little later, he bade him come to Nicopolis in Macedonia, where he intended himself to pass the winter ('Titus iii. 12). The only later mention of him in Scripture is that during St. Paul's second imprisonment at Rome he was preaching in Dalmatia, and apparently had gone thither from Rome (2 Tim. iv. 10). He afterwards returned to Crete, where he is said to have died in the ninety-fourth year of his age.

SYLVANUS is another form of the name Silas. He is first mentioned in Acts xv. 22, when he was one of those, called "chief men among the brethren," chosen to carry the decision of the Council of Jerusalem to Antioch. He is also called a "prophet" (Acts xv. 32). He remained at Antioch at that time, and soon afterwards accompanied St. Paul on his missionary journey through Syria and Asia Minor to Macedonia (Acts xv. 34, 40 and xvi. 1–11). Though he was a Roman citizen (Acts xvi. 37), he was scourged and imprisoned with St. Paul at Philippi; but being released accompanied the apostle to Thessalonica and Berea. When the Jews stirred up a tumult against St. Paul in the latter city, he departed, leaving Silas and Timothy behind (xvii. 14), who soon afterwards rejoined him at Corinth (xviii. 5). Consequently, when St. Paul shortly afterwards wrote his two Epistles to the Thessalonians from Corinth, Silas, or Sylvanus, as well as Timothy, are joined with him in the salutations (1 Thess. i. 1 and 2 Thess. i. 1). Nothing is known of his later life, unless he be the same person as the Silvanus mentioned in 1 Pet. v. 12.

## CHAPTER III.

### THE CHURCH OF CORINTH.

1. THE CITY OF CORINTH was one of the leading cities of Greece. Its position on an isthmus between two seas made it always a great centre of commerce; and it had two ports, Lechæum on the Western, and Cenchrea on the Eastern, Sea. It was taken and pillaged by the

Roman general L. Mummius in the year 146 B.C., but it was rebuilt by Julius Cæsar (B.C. 44), and became the capital of the Roman proconsular province of Achaia. It soon recovered its former mercantile importance and its wealth. Along with its riches, Corinth was always noted for a degree of luxury and impurity, which became proverbial even in the pagan Roman Empire. It was famous also as a seat of philosophy and of literature, and as the scene of the Isthmian Games.

2. FOUNDATION OF THE CHURCH OF CORINTH. St. Paul's first visit to this city was made about the year 51 A.D., in the course of his second missionary journey (Acts xviii. 1–18). Here he spent eighteen months, and founded a church, and made a considerable number of converts. These were mostly from among the poor and unlearned ("there are not many wise according to the flesh, not many mighty, not many noble," 1 Cor. i. 26). There were, however, some richer men among them, such as may have been Crispus, the ruler of the synagogue (Acts xviii. 8), and Erastus, the treasurer of the city (Rom. xvi. 23). At least it appears from 2 Cor. viii. 14, &c., that they were wealthy by comparison with the Christians at Jerusalem. It is evident also that, in spite of some exceptions, the greater part of the converts were Gentiles (1 Cor. xii. 2—"when you were heathens").

3. RISE OF FACTIONS IN THE CORINTHIAN CHURCH. After St. Paul had spent a year and a half at Corinth, he returned (A.D. 53) to Antioch; and shortly afterwards set out on his third missionary journey, in which he spent more than two years (A.D. 55–57) at Ephesus. During this time it is very probable that he crossed the Ægean Sea to pay a second short visit to Corinth (see Appendix I.). In any case it is certain that before St. Paul reached Ephesus, Corinth was visited by Apollo, an Alexandrine Jew and a recent convert. He was an eloquent and fervent man, and learned in the Jewish Scriptures, which he employed to convince the Corinthian Jews and to strengthen the

Faith in that city (cf. Acts xviii. 24—xix. 1). As he had received most of his Christian instruction from Aquila and Priscilla, who were St. Paul's converts, it is not probable that his teaching had anything to do with causing the factions which soon arose to trouble that Church, although it is evident that his name was afterwards made use of by one of the parties which arose there (cf. 1 Cor. i. 12). After his departure there came to Corinth certain Jewish teachers (2 Cor. xi. 22), who strove to create a schism in the Corinthian Church. It is not known exactly what their teaching was. The opinion that it was necessary for Gentile converts to keep the ceremonial Jewish law had been made formally heretical by the decision of the Council of Jerusalem (Acts xv. 1–29); and, as there is no reference to this subject in either of the Epistles to the Corinthians, it is most likely that they did not explicitly teach this heresy. Nor is there any evidence that they openly taught, like some other Judaizers after the Council of Jerusalem, that though the law was not binding on the Gentiles, it was yet better for them to follow it. They seem to have attempted to disparage St. Paul's authority rather than his doctrine, hoping, probably, that if the first were overthrown it would be easy to destroy the latter. They came to Corinth with letters of commendation (2 Cor. iii. 1), on the strength of which they professed to be representatives of St. Peter, and to teach his doctrine (1 Cor. i. 12). They denied that St. Paul was an apostle, or at least that he was as much an apostle as the original Twelve, on the ground that he had not seen our Lord in the flesh, as they had. They even pointed to the fact that St. Paul received no pay from the Corinthians as evidence that he was conscious of not being a true apostle, and they used every means to disparage his character and his work.

4. THE FIRST EPISTLE TO THE CORINTHIANS. Whilst St. Paul was at Ephesus he sent an Epistle to the Corinthians (cf. 1 Cor. v. 9), which has perished. It was apparently from their reply to this that he learned of the schismatic spirit and other corruptions which existed

amongst them, and which he at once strove to correct by the Epistle known as the First to the Corinthians, written probably about Easter, A.D. 57 In this Epistle he refers to the contentions which he had heard of as existing amongst them (i. 10-13), and exhorts them to unity. He claims to be a true apostle, and to have seen our Lord (ix. 1, and xv. 8-11). He shows the error of those who esteem the human wisdom rather than the Divine authority of their teachers (i. 17-31); and while he acknowledges his lack of eloquence (ii. 1-6), he claims to be truly endowed with the Holy Ghost (7-16). He shows the foolishness of their schisms by the fact that all the teachers among whom they were divided were alike ministers of Christ (ch. iii., esp. 3-10, 21, 22): yet he contrasts the false teachers with the true apostles (iv. 6-13), and shows that the primary obedience of the Corinthians is due to himself as their founder (14-16), and declares that, if necessary, he will vindicate his authority (18-21). He also explains his true reasons for not accepting money from them (ix. 1-18).

5. OTHER EVENTS PRECEDING THE SECOND EPISTLE. Before writing his First Epistle to the Corinthians St. Paul had sent Timothy and Erastus to go through Macedonia to Corinth, in order to prepare the way for the visit which he intended to make himself to that city, by removing the contentions there (cf. Acts xix. 22; 1 Cor. iv. 17, xvi. 10). Before he heard of the contentions at Corinth his intention seems to have been to go direct to Corinth by sea from Ephesus, but when he had heard of the scandals in that Church he changed his mind, and decided to travel first through Macedonia (1 Cor. xvi. 5-7; 2 Cor. i. 15, 16). Soon after the dispatch of the First Epistle St. Paul sent Titus to Corinth, apparently to ascertain the effect which that letter had had on the Corinthians (cf. 2 Cor. vii. 6-8). Both Timothy and Titus had rejoined St. Paul before the date of his Second Epistle (2 Cor. i. 1, and vii. 6).

## CHAPTER IV.

### THE SECOND EPISTLE TO THE CORINTHIANS.

1. OCCASION AND OBJECT OF WRITING THIS EPISTLE. It is not certain whether, at the time he sent Titus to Corinth, St. Paul intended to await his return at Ephesus. But whatever his intentions were, the tumult caused by Demetrius (Acts xix. 23–xx. 1) compelled him to leave Ephesus. He proceeded to Troas, hoping to meet Titus there (2 Cor. ii. 12), but as he did not find him he proceeded to Macedonia, where he at last met him (2 Cor. vii. 6). The news he received from Titus was that the incestuous man, who had been excommunicated in the First Epistle (1 Cor. v.), was now penitent, and that most of the Corinthians had submitted and repented of their evil deeds (2 Cor. vii. 7, &c.). Nevertheless his opponents were only the more enraged by his reproofs, and were using all means to bring him into odium among the Corinthians. Besides this he heard that the collection for the poor at Jerusalem, which they had been prepared to make in the previous year, and of which he had reminded them in his former letter (xvi. 1-3), had not yet been made. He therefore judged it necessary, before he visited them himself, to send them another letter. In this he gives an indulgence to the penitent (ii. 5-11), and exhorts them to promptitude in making the collection (viii., ix.); but above all he vindicates his apostolic authority, exculpates himself from all the charges of the Judaizers, and calls on those who still cling to these false teachers no longer to allow themselves to be misled

2. PLACE AND TIME OF WRITING. It is certain that this letter was written from Macedonia. The subscription in some MSS. says it was written at Philippi, but this is doubtful, since (in viii. 1) St. Paul speaks as though he had visited several Churches in Macedonia, whereas Philippi was the first that he would reach. It was written a few months after Pentecost, and (according to

most chronologists) in the year A.D. 57. It was carried to Corinth by Titus and two other disciples (viii. 16-24).

3. AUTHORSHIP AND INTEGRITY. There has never been among Catholics the least doubt with regard to either of these points. The Epistle has been received without question from the earliest ages. And so fully does it bear the marks of genuineness that no modern rationalist has ventured seriously to dispute its authorship. A few of the modern critics have attempted to show that this letter is a combination of two or three original Epistles, but they have had scarcely any followers.

4. ARGUMENT OF THE EPISTLE. St. Paul has before him the task of exculpating himself from the false charges of his opponents, amongst others that of dilatoriness in coming to them, and, at the same time, he has to reprove his converts for certain faults which they have not yet amended. Accordingly he considers that his best excuse lies in a plain narrative of the facts, in telling everything just as it happened ; and that the best way to prepare them for receiving reproof profitably is by alluding first to those matters in which he was able to praise them, by reviving their loyalty towards himself as their spiritual father, and by appealing to their generosity in God's service. This accordingly is the order which he follows, as will be seen from the summaries prefixed to each of the three parts into which the Epistle is divided.

## CHAPTER V.

### THE TEXT OF THIS EPISTLE.

1. GREEK. The oldest Greek manuscripts of the New Testament are the following :—

(i) The Sinaitic (denoted by the Hebrew letter א, Aleph), recently discovered, and now kept at St. Petersburg. It is of the *fourth* century, and contains the New Testament entire.

(ii) The Alexandrine (known as A), presented to Charles I. in 1628, by the Patriarch of Alexandria, and now in the British Museum. It is of the *fifth* century, and contains the New Testament with some omissions. In this Epistle it is defective from chap. iv. 13 to xii. 6. inclusive.

(iii) The Vatican (B), preserved in the Vatican Library. It is of the *fourth* century, and contains this Epistle entire, as well as the greater part of the New Testament.

(iv) The Codex Ephræmi (C), now at Paris. It contains fragments of both Testaments and is assigned to the *fifth* century. Of this Epistle it contains the portion from chap. i. 2 to x. 8.

(v) The Codex Claromontanus (D), at Paris. It contains the whole of this Epistle, and, with the exception of a few verses, all the Epistles of St. Paul. It is assigned to the *sixth* century. It must be distinguished from the Codex Bezæ, which is denoted by the same letter (D), and which contains only the Gospels and Acts.

The Greek, when quoted in this edition, is usually taken from the Vatican manuscript, which is the one generally regarded by scholars as the most reliable.

2. LATIN. The Vulgate translation was made by St. Jerome about the year 383. It is a revision of the older Latin version, known as the Vetus Latina, compared with Greek MSS. older than any which now exist. The edition of this version which is now in use was published by authority of Pope Clement VIII. in 1592.

3. ENGLISH. All English Catholic versions of the Bible are necessarily translations of the Vulgate, which is the authorized version in use in the Church. All modern translations are based upon that made at Rheims in 1582.

This was revised three times by Bishop Challoner between 1749 and 1752. In these versions something was done to correct errors in the translation, but more care was taken in removing archaisms, and in adapting the translation to the flowing style in vogue at that period. Several subsequent revisions have been made, but no one of them has been of sufficient excellence to win for itself universal adoption.

The text here adopted, not because it is the best, but because it is the most convenient, is that of the sixpenny New Testament published by the firm of Burns and Oates. This text is a combination of the first two of Challoner's versions, and has been chosen both because it is the version most familiar to Catholics, and also because, if not better, it is at any rate not, on the whole, demonstrably inferior to any of the other versions in circulation. If it be compared with other translations, it will be found that those which are superior in one passage are not so good in another. One example from this Epistle will illustrate this. In viii. 10 our version translates *ab anno priore* by *a year ago*, instead of (as it should be) *since the preceding year*. But in ix. 2 a similar phrase is rightly translated. Some later revisions which have corrected the error in the first passage have introduced it into the second.

Under these circumstances, though a new translation is certainly in many ways to be desired, it does not seem that any of the other versions in existence has any such distinct and uniform superiority over this as would justify us in giving it the preference.

The whole subject of the texts of the New Testament will be found more fully treated by Mgr. Ward in an article which at present forms a part of the Introduction to his commentary on St. Luke's Gospel.

# THE SECOND EPISTLE OF ST. PAUL TO THE CORINTHIANS.

## PART I., CHAPS. I.–VII.

*SUMMARY.*

### VINDICATION OF HIS APOSTOLIC AUTHORITY.

| | |
|---|---:|
| PREFACE . . . . . . . . . . | i. 1, 2 |
| A. *He asserts his true love for his spiritual children—* i. 3–ii. 17 | |
|   (i) By a general reference to his troubles gladly undergone for their sakes . . . | i. 3–7 |
|   (ii) By a special allusion to his tribulation in Asia, which led him more than ever to put his confidence, after God, in their prayers, and so made their love and trust of one another reciprocal . . . . . . | 8 14 |
|   (iii) He shows that his reason for not coming to them before visiting Macedonia was that he did not wish to be obliged to pain them by exercising his apostolic authority with severity | i. 15–ii. 4 |
|   (iv) He now exercises this authority to give an indulgence to the excommunicated man, trusting in their obedience to carry it out . . | 5–11 |
|   (v) He shows how his love and anxiety for them caused him no rest, until he received good news of them . . . . . . | 12, 13 |
|   (vi) He does all his works for their sakes, and for the glory of God . . . . . . | 14–17 |

## II. TO THE CORINTHIANS.

*He magnifies his ministry*—iii. 1-vi. 10
- (i) His office indeed needs no exaltation; it is made known to all by its fruits in the amendment of the Corinthians. . . . . iii. 1-3
- (ii) And in exalting it, he exalts, not himself, but God, whose grace alone gave him apostolic power . . . . . . . . 4-6
- (iii) The ministry of the Old Testament was indeed glorified with a reflection of the Divine glory, but its glory was temporary and imperfect; that of the New Testament is full of a lasting glory, the true glory of God Himself, which shines from the face of JESUS. . . . iii. 7-iv. 6
- (iv) This ministry he exercises as the partner of Christ, not only in His glory, but also in His mortification and suffering, which all must share in time who would share His life in eternity . iv. 7-18
- (v) But all this is undergone for their sakes; and the consideration of these eternal things (v. 1-10) urges him to seek nothing but the glory of God and the good of their souls (v. 11-vi. 2), despising all earthly sufferings (vi. 3-10) . . . . . . . v. 1-vi. 10

C. *He appeals to the Corinthians to show generosity in God's service, and not to cavil at His ministers; and at the same time rejoices in the progress they have made in penance*- vi. 11-vii. 16
- (i) He calls on them to separate themselves from the wicked and infidels . . . . . vi. 11-vii. 1
- (ii) And to receive the apostle and his companions, whose only aim is for God, and whose joy is to find them faithful, as he did when Titus came to Macedonia, and reported well of them . vii. 2-7
- (iii) He rejoices at their true penitence, and does not hesitate (as a false apostle would) to cause them sorrow in order to their amendment . . 8-16

# CHAPTER I.

PAUL an apostle of JESUS CHRIST by the will of God, and Timothy *our* brother: to the Church of God that is at Corinth, with all the saints that are in all Achaia: Grace unto you and peace from God our ₂ Father and from the Lord JESUS CHRIST.

## CHAPTER I.

**1.** *an apostle of* JESUS CHRIST *by the will of God.* St. Paul begins by asserting that he had received the office of apostle by God's will, a fact which had been denied by some of those who were trying to create a schism in the Corinthian Church by denying St. Paul's apostolic authority. See Introduction, chap. iii. 3.

**2.** *Timothy* had recently returned from Corinth, whither he had been sent by St. Paul from Ephesus (Acts xix. 22). See Introduction, chap. ii.

*our brother.* Timothy is called here *brother* not merely because of the communion of faith, in which sense all the faithful are brethren. Here the expression is more particular and emphatic, and marks out St. Timothy as a sharer in St. Paul's apostolic labours, though of course he was far inferior to the apostle himself. St. Thomas compares this with the custom observed by the Pope of addressing all bishops as "brethren."

St. Timothy is united with St. Paul in the salutation only, not in the composition of the Epistle.

*Corinth* was the metropolis of Achaia, and its Church had been founded by St. Paul himself, who had spent eighteen months there. (See Introduction, iii.) It was the custom for epistles directed to one Church to be read there publicly during the Mass, and then forwarded to neighbouring Churches, which would take copies of them for preservation. In Achaia, however, no other Churches are known to have existed at this time, and the apostle probably refers only to scattered Christians.

*saints.* The term "*saints*" is frequently applied in the New Testament to all the faithful—both because they are sanctified in baptism, and also because of the profession of their lives, and the ideal at which they are bound to aim.

*God.* As God the Father corresponds most naturally to the idea of

Blessed be the God and Father of our Lord JESUS CHRIST, the Father of mercies, and the God of all comfort, who comforteth us in all our tribulation; that we also may be able to comfort them who are in all distress, by the exhortation wherewith we also are exhorted by God. For as the sufferings of Christ abound in us: so also

God as revealed to the Jews, so St. Paul commonly refers only to Him when he uses the name of God. (There are, however, some exceptions, as Rom. ix. 5; Tit. ii. 13; iii. 4.) The divinity of our Lord seems to be here implied, in His being coupled with the Father as the source of grace and peace.

**3.** *the God and Father of* . . . God the Father is Father of our Lord in His Divine nature, because of His eternal generation, and "God of our Lord JESUS CHRIST" in His human nature because this owes its being to God as to its Creator and Preserver. For this reason our Lord cried out from the Cross, "My God, My God, why hast Thou forsaken Me?" and after His resurrection He said to His disciples, "I ascend to My Father and your Father, to My God and your God." In His humanity He adored the Divine Father by prayer, and observance of the Jewish law, and by submitting His human will to the will of His Divine Father (cf. Matt. xxvi. 39; John iv. 34, xv. 10; Rom. xv. 3). According to some commentators there is a different meaning in the use of this phrase. As the Jews spoke of the "God of Abraham, of Isaac, and of Jacob," in reference to the revelation of Himself which God had made through those patriarchs to the Jews, so the apostle may here intend to speak of the God who has revealed Himself to Christians through JESUS CHRIST (cf. Eph. i. 3, 17; 1 Pet. i. 3).

*Father of mercies* may mean only "*merciful Father*" according to the Hebrew idiom; but more probably, followed as it is by "*God of all comfort,*" it means that God distributes His mercies amongst men like a good Father.

*the God of all comfort.* The words translated "*comfort,*" "*comforteth,*" "*exhortation,*" "*consolation,*" in *vv.* 3–7, are in Greek the same word, (παρακαλέω, παράκλησις), or from the same root. It is not easy to render it into Latin or English by a single word, but "*exhort*" is nearer than "*comfort*" to the meaning of the Greek, which is rather "*to call upon*" us and "*to encourage*" us to make efforts, than "*to afford us consolation.*" It is rendered very well by Bp. McEvilly, "*call on us to assume courage.*" St. Chrysostom says that to be thus comforted is a greater benefit than not to be allowed to suffer adversity; because it both shows the power of God, and increases the patience of the sufferers.

**4.** *that we also may be able* . . . St. Paul, in his humility and his zeal, considers the consolation he receives as given, not for his own merit, but to enable him to help others by sympathy.

**5.** *the sufferings of Christ abound in us.* Some commentator by Christ doth our comfort abound.  Now whether we **6** be in tribulation, *it is* for your exhortation and salvation: or whether we be comforted, *it is* for your consolation: or whether we be exhorted, *it is* for your exhortation and salvation, which worketh the enduring of the same sufferings which we also suffer.  That our **7**

suppose that the expression "*the sufferings of Christ*" means only sufferings endured for the name of Christ; but it is better to interpret it as meaning that the sufferings of the just for the name of Christ belong truly to Christ Himself, who suffers in His members.  This truth was the first of the facts of faith which St. Paul learned, when, on his way to Damascus to persecute the Church, our Lord appeared to him saying, "*Saul, Saul, why persecutest thou Me?*" (Acts ix. 4).  St. Anselm, following this interpretation, says that hardships which have to be borne are rightly called the sufferings of Christ, because they were first endured by Christ, and then transmitted by Him to His faithful for them to endure.  This interpretation also agrees best with the Greek, which means rather abound or overflow "*unto us*" than "*in us*," that is, the sufferings of Christ are passed on to His followers, who have to bear the Cross after Him, or rather *with* Him, and *in* Him (cf. Col. i. 24).

*by Christ*—rather "*through Christ.*"  Christ affords the consolation as God, which He has merited by suffering as man.

**6.** *whether we be comforted* . . .  The Greek here in the manuscripts which we possess does not quite correspond to our translation.  The Greek has only two clauses in place of three.  As explained above, the words translated "*exhortation*" and "*consolation*" are the same in Greek, and the second clause may be translated thus: "*or whether we be $\binom{comforted}{exhorted}$ it is for your $\binom{consolation}{exhortation}$ which . . .*"  It is probable that this one clause was expanded into two by the translator, so as to more fully express the Greek.

*which worketh*—that is, *your consolation and hope of salvation give you courage to endure with patience.*  The words may, however, also be rendered, "*which is effected by,*" i.e., consolation and salvation are the result of the endurance of suffering.  The faithful are to be encouraged (1) by the tribulations of the apostle, which ought to inspire them both in enduring their own lighter sufferings and in working out their salvation (cf. Heb. xii. 1-6); (2) by his consolations, which enable him better to encourage them, and which lead them to hope for similar consolations if they are patient under suffering.

**7.** *partakers of the sufferings:* either by undergoing persecutions and hardships themselves, or, more probably, by their sympathy with his sufferings.

hope for you may be steadfast: knowing that as you are partakers of the sufferings, so shall you be also of the consolation.

8 For we would not have you ignorant, brethren, of our tribulation which came to us in Asia, that we were pressed out of measure above our strength, so that we were weary 9 even of life. But we had in ourselves the answer of death, 10 that we should not trust in ourselves, but in God who raiseth the dead, who hath delivered and doth deliver us out of so great dangers: in whom we trust that he will yet

8 *Asia*—i.e., the Roman province of Asia of which Ephesus was the capital. It comprised Mysia, Lydia, and Caria; the western portion of Asia Minor.

*our tribulation.* There has been much dispute as to what is here referred to. We learn from Acts (chap. xix.) that St. Paul spent three years in Ephesus, making many converts (see *vv.* 17-20), until a certain Demetrius stirred up an agitation against him among the silver-smiths, and afterwards created a riot in the city. In this riot, however, the apostle seems not to have been harmed, and apparently he left Ephesus very shortly afterwards. That he expected both his success and the opposition to him appears from 1 Cor. xvi. 8, 9. This incident, however, scarcely seems sufficient to warrant so strong a reference. We are left to suppose either—(1) That this riot was much more serious than the narrative in the Acts would lead us to believe; or (2) that he refers to the whole opposition he encountered during his stay at Ephesus, and that he intends to imply that he lived in constant danger of his life, possibly from some secret plot formed by the idol-makers; or (3) that he alludes to something nowhere else referred to. In this latter case the following verses seem to suggest that it was probably some illness.

*pressed,* that is, "*weighed down*" (Lat. "gravati").

*we were weary.* The Greek (ὥστε ἐξαπορηθῆναι ἡμᾶς καὶ τοῦ ζῆν) means rather "*we were at a loss how to preserve our life.*" These words seem to confirm the idea of a plot rather than an illness.

9. *We had in ourselves the answer of death* (τὸ ἀπόκριμα τοῦ θανάτου), i.e., *the expectation of death.* The *answer* is that which his own judgment gave when he considered the danger in which he was placed. He came to the conclusion that he had no hope of preserving his life, at least so far as its preservation was dependent upon his own efforts. God had allowed him to be brought to a condition apparently hopeless, so that he might learn not to trust to himself, but only to the omnipotence of God, who never had failed him in the past, and never would fail him in the future.

*who raiseth the dead.* He considered himself as being past all human aid, and his deliverance was therefore to be looked upon as being as great an exercise of Divine power, as raising the dead.

also deliver us; you helping withal in prayer for us: that for this gift obtained for us, by the means of many persons, thanks may be given by many in our behalf. For our glory is this, the testimony of our conscience, that in simplicity of heart and sincerity of God, and not in carnal wisdom, but in the grace of God, we have conversed in this world: and more abundantly towards you. For we write no other things to you than what you have read and known. And I hope that you shall know unto the end: as also you have known us in part, that we are your glory, as you also are ours in the day of our Lord JESUS CHRIST.

**11.** *you helping in prayer for us.* St. Paul's confidence in God does not prevent him from asking the prayers of the Corinthians, but rather leads him to do so. He asks them not to cease praying, and at the same time to give thanks for his deliverance. We see how far the apostle is from those in the sixteenth century who professed to revive his teaching, but who asserted that to ask the prayers of men was a derogation from the glory of God.

**12.** *for our glory is this.* The connection between this verse and what has preceded is a little difficult to see. St. Chrysostom thinks that St. Paul wishes to warn his readers against thinking that God's graces are to be expected by those, who merely commend themselves to the prayers of others, while they are themselves idle. It is more probable, perhaps, that he is anticipating a possible argument of his detractors at Corinth, who might say that his sufferings were deserved, and sent as a Divine punishment.

*the testimony of our conscience* . . . Cf. 1 John iii. 21, 22, where that apostle teaches that a pure conscience is most important for obtaining our petitions.

*carnal wisdom.* His detractors said that he was not learned nor eloquent (x. 10). His reply, in effect, is that human wisdom is not valued by him in comparison with grace. He was, however, by no means devoid of learning, for he had studied under Gamaliel, one of the most learned Rabbis of the day—and the governor Festus ascribed his zeal to madness caused by over-study (cf. Acts xxvi. 24).

*we have conversed.* The English word "*conversed*" is obsolete in this sense. The meaning is, "*We behaved ourselves in this world.*"

**13.** *we write no other things* . . . St. Paul defends his sincerity and consistency by saying that he writes nothing but what they both read in his letters and recognize in his life, and which he hopes that they may continue to do, as they have (partially, at least) done hitherto. His writing, their reading, and their knowledge of him, that is to say, his words, his meaning, and his life, are all consistent with one another.

**14.** *in part.* This implies either—(1) They had not fully recognized

15 And in this confidence I had a mind to come to you
16 before, that you might have a second grace: and to pass by you into Macedonia, and again from Macedonia to come to you, and by you to be brought on my way towards Judea.
17 Whereas then I was thus minded, did I use lightness? Or the things that I purpose, do I purpose according to the flesh, that there should be with me, *It is*, and *It is*

his sincerity, as was shown by their listening to his detractors; or (2) St. Paul is speaking modestly, suggesting that the Corinthians could only have observed in him the virtues mentioned in *v.* 12 in a very imperfect form. The former interpretation, however, appears best to agree with the context.

*we are your glory* . . . that is, they acknowledge his claims by the fact that they glory in having had him as their founder.

*in the day of our Lord* JESUS CHRIST, that is, in the Day of Judgment, when all vain glory will be exposed.

**15.** *in this confidence*—i.e., in the confidence he had that they were his glory, that they were a credit to him.

*I had a mind* . . . Was this intention of visiting Corinth before going to Macedonia prior or subsequent to the writing of the First Epistle, in which he says he will only come to Corinth, when he has passed through Macedonia (cf. 1 Cor. xvi. 5-7)? St. Ambrose and St. Anselm both suppose that at the time he wrote the First Epistle, in which he had to rebuke them for many things, he was determined only to visit them once; but that, when he heard of their repentance, he formed the resolution here referred to, but which he again reversed, as he explains in *v.* 23. This supposition would explain the necessity of his exculpating himself from the charge of fickleness. Nevertheless it seems simpler to suppose, with St. Thomas Aquinas and Cajetan, that the intention here alluded to was his original design, which he had abandoned when he wrote the First Epistle. If so, it is very possible that he had communicated his first intention to them in that letter, no longer extant, which is referred to in 1 Cor. v. 9.

*a second grace.* See Appendix I.

**16.** *towards Judea.* When he wrote the First Epistle St. Paul did not know where he would go to from Corinth (cf. 1 Cor. xvi. 6); but it appears that in the meantime he had received an inspiration bidding him to proceed to Jerusalem (Acts xix. 21). Nevertheless he was prevented from actually sailing direct to Syria (Acts xx. 3), and consequently returned to Macedonia and took ship at Philippi.

**17.** *according to the flesh* may mean either (1) following a mere whim or inclination, and not the guidance of reason; or (2) being led only by human reason, with no regard to Divine inspiration. The former, however, seems to suit the context better, because the determination to visit them is defended against the charge of imprudence; but it *not?* But God is faithful, for our preaching which was to 18 you, was not *It is*, and *It is not*. For the Son of God, 19 JESUS CHRIST, who was preached among you by us, by me and Silvanus and Timothy, was not, *It is*, and *It is not*, but *It is*, was in him. For all the promises of God are in 20 him, *It is*: therefore also by him, *Amen* to God, unto our glory. Now he that confirmeth us with you in Christ, and 21

would be less easy to maintain that the resolution was Divinely inspired, seeing that he did not adhere to it.

*that there should be* . . . St. Chrysostom explains this passage thus: St. Paul says he is not to be accused of fickleness in changing his intention; he did not abandon the wish, but subjected it to the Divine inspiration, which bade him do what he had not thought of previously. Thus there was no change at all in his own intention to visit Corinth first, but he had been prevented by his obedience to the Holy Ghost from carrying it out. This explanation agrees very well with the words of St. Paul in this place; for he appears to deny any change in his purpose; and it is only in this sense that it is possible to make this assertion. Many commentators offer a slightly different explanation by supposing that St. Paul does not deny a change in his own intention, but only that such a change was inconsiderate or fraudulent.

**18.** *God is faithful.* This may be a form of calling God to witness, meaning, "*I call on God as my faithful witness that my preaching* . . ." But a better interpretation is. "*Our preaching was as sincere and unchanging as God, who was its subject.*" He supposes that his enemies may say that if he changed his purpose of visiting them, he may also find reasons for changing his teaching, like the heretics of all ages, whose teaching is ever changing and inconsistent, or, as it is called in our own times, "progressive." To meet this objection St. Paul answers that his teaching is absolutely one and unchangeable, since it is the very truth of God, the selfsame immutable Revelation made by His own Son, not through St. Paul alone, but through all the ministers of His Church.

**19.** *Silvanus.* See Introduction, chap. ii.; cf. Acts xviii. 5.

**20.** *all the promises.* A better translation of the Latin and of the Greek would be, "*The promises of God, however many they be.*"

*are in Him, It is* . . . i.e., God's promises are unchangeable and fixed in our Lord, who as God brings them to completion, and as man merits their fulfilment. Therefore also by Him *Amen* can be said to God Himself in ratification of these promises.

*unto our glory.* The Greek is "*unto glory through us.*" The meaning is that the promises of God declared through us can be accepted as true and ratified by the saying "*Amen*," and this act of faith will redound to the glory of God.

**21.** *now he that confirmeth us.* . . . The connection of this verse with what precedes seems to be that St. Paul wishes to declare the

22 that hath anointed us, is God: Who also hath sealed us,
23 and given the pledge of the Spirit in our hearts. But I call God to witness upon my soul, that to spare you, I

immutability of God's promises not only in themselves, but also in his own presentation of them; and to do this it is necessary to establish his Divine authority. As God is in Himself "It is," that is to say, stable, so He makes His ministers the same, and affords both them and their hearers the gift of a strong faith to enable them to adhere to these truths.

*in Christ*, whose members we become by Baptism, and in whom we inhere by faith.

*hath anointed . . . hath sealed . . . given.* These verbs are in Greek the aorist, and therefore should be translated "*anointed . . . sealed . . . gave.*"

*anointed*, that is, by the gifts of the Holy Ghost, which are typified by unction. That the unction of the Holy Ghost keeps us in the Truth is seen also from 1 John ii. 20–27.

*sealed.* The graces, especially the miraculous powers, which he received from God, marked him as God's duly accredited apostle.

*pledge.* The word means a small part of a gift, given as an assurance of the rest. This pledge is therefore, as St. Anselm says, the gift by which our soul is strengthened to the certainty of interior hope (cf. also Eph. i. 14). It does not, of course, amount to an absolute assurance of our salvation. St. Chrysostom explains *vv.* 21, 22 as meaning that God confirms His promises by giving His grace as a pledge of future benefits, by which grace He anoints us and seals us as His sons. Some commentators suppose that both verses refer to the graces bestowed in Baptism. Others, again, see a reference to Confirmation, which in those days was administered immediately after Baptism; for in Confirmation our faith is strengthened and confirmed, we receive the unction of charity and of grace, we have a pledge of future glory, and are sealed with that character imprinted on the soul, by which we are made the servants and the soldiers of God. But though it is probable that this Sacrament was in the apostle's mind, the context seems to require a reference to some gifts more *visible* than the ordinary sacramental grace, such, for example, as miracles or tongues, which might attest his authority. And we know that in the first ages such extraordinary gifts frequently did accompany the conferring of the Sacraments, especially that of Confirmation (cf. Acts xix. 6), and were possessed in an eminent degree by St. Paul (cf. 1 Cor. xiv. 18; Acts xix. 11, 12, xx. 9–12, &c.).

**23.** *I call God to witness upon my soul*—i.e., if I lie, to take vengeance upon my soul.

*to spare you*, that is, in the hope that, if he allowed time, their repentance would be complete: for if he had gone to Corinth earlier he would have been obliged to punish (cf. xiii. 2, 10).

*not because we exercise dominion over your faith* (οὐχ ὅτι κυριεύομεν came not any more to Corinth, not because we exercise dominion over your faith : but we are helpers of your joy : for in faith you stand.

## CHAPTER II.

BUT I determined this with myself, not to come to you again in sorrow. For if I make you sorrowful, 2 who is he then that can make me glad, but the same who

ἡμῶν τῆς πίστεως). The word κυριεύομεν denotes the power of a master over his slaves. The false apostles, who were calumniating St. Paul among the Corinthians, were themselves taking advantage of their faith to exercise over them a tyranny of this kind (cf. xi. 19, 20). The authority of a true apostle, on the other hand, is that of a father (1 Cor. iv. 14. 15). This spiritual fatherhood involves the power of admonishing, of commanding, of threatening, and of punishing, like the human fatherhood, which is a shadow of it. These powers are in effect claimed by St. Paul in this verse, for he who spares must have the right of punishing, and they are constantly exercised by him upon occasion (cf. xiii. 2. 10; x. 6; 1 Cor. iv. 14, 21 ; v. 3-5 ; &c.). But this legitimate authority is exercised for the good of the faithful (xiii. 10), not to satisfy any ambition, like that claimed by the false apostles. Some commentators understand these words to mean "we do not compel faith," because faith is of free will and cannot be forced. But though this makes good sense, it does not suit the context, in which there is no question of forcing faith upon them.

*helpers of your joy.* Though it is true he has been obliged to admonish and punish the Corinthians, yet it has not been his desire to make them sorrowful, and even his admonitions have brought them that joy which comes from penitence.

*for in faith you stand.* That is to say, *in faith you are steadfast;* and therefore, even if their morals needed correction, he hoped that they would receive his admonitions with respect to that, without making it necessary for him to resort to severity.

### CHAPTER II.

1. *again.* See Appendix I.
*in sorrow.* If St. Paul had come sooner he would have felt sorrow at their impenitence, and he would have been obliged also to cause the Corinthians sorrow by his admonitions.

2. *if I make you sorrowful.* . . . St. Paul's meaning in this verse is : *If I cause you sorrow, this is necessary for you and for me, for he who is led to penitence by my admonitions will give me joy : and if I were not now to pain you by my admonitions, and so lead you to a true sorrow for sin, I could not be made glad: nor would you have*

3 is made sorrowful by me? And I wrote this same to you; that I may not, when I come, have sorrow upon sorrow, from them of whom I ought to rejoice; having confidence
4 in you all that my joy is the joy of you all. For out of much affliction and anguish of heart I wrote to you with many tears; not that you should be made sorrowful, but that you might know the charity I have more abundantly towards you.
5 And if any one have caused grief, he hath not grieved

*any real joy, because not only would you have a bad conscience, but also I have confidence that as "my joy is the joy of you all," so would my sorrow be your sorrow also.*

**3.** *I wrote this same to you.* That is to say, *I declared in my first Epistle this intention of not visiting you till after my visit to Macedonia.*

*my joy is the joy of you all.* This makes him confident that they will reform before he comes.

**4.** *not that you should be made sorrowful.* St. Paul does not mean that in writing his first Epistle he had no desire to cause them sorrow; for he rebuked them for not mourning (1 Cor. v. 2); but the sorrow which he wished to produce in them was not sorrow for its own sake, but that of penance (cf. vii. 9-11).

*charity.* True charity consists, not in passing over faults, but in boldly correcting them, provided this correction proceeds from a desire for the highest good of the sinner, and not from any malice.

**5-11.** St. Paul considers the case of the man guilty of incest, whom he had previously ordered to be excommunicated (cf. 1 Cor. v.). This excommunication, in addition to his exclusion from the Holy Communion, and from the services of the Church, involved also separation from the company of the faithful (1 Cor. v. 11), and apparently bodily sufferings inflicted by Satan (*ibid. v.* 5). As the man has since repented, the apostle now bids them remit the remainder of his punishment, which has not yet been fully undergone (*v.* 7), and confirms this remission by the authority of Christ, whose representative he is (*v.* 10).

**5.** *and if any one have caused grief.* . . . This verse may be translated thus: "*If any one have caused grief he hath grieved not me, but (in part, that I press not too heavily) all of you.*" The meaning is, *he has not grieved me alone* (or *me in particular*), *but also all of you to some extent—I will not say altogether, lest I should seem to exaggerate his offence, if I were to exaggerate the grief it caused.* It has been interpreted by others thus: *He hath not grieved me except partially; for to say that I was wholly grieved would be to burden you all with the charge of complicity in his sin, whereas in truth the conduct of many of you has done much to mitigate my grief.* Or again: *I say only partially, for to use a stronger term would cause you too much sorrow, since I know that my sorrow is yours.* But the first inter-

me; but in part, that I may not burden you all. To him 6
that is such a one this rebuke is sufficient, that is given by
many: so that contrariwise you should rather pardon and 7
comfort him, lest perhaps such an one be swallowed up

pretation, which is adopted by almost all commentators, both Latin and Greek, is quite in accordance with the text, and gives the best sense. A slight modification of the explanation of this translation, which is perhaps an improvement, is to take it as meaning, *also partially* (*for I will not blame you too much by denying absolutely that you had any grief at his offence*) *all of you*.

6. *rebuke.* The word thus translated means properly, "*penalty.*" It refers to the expulsion of the man from the Church by excommunication, and also to his exclusion from the society of the faithful.

*many.* It is possible that this ought to be translated, "*the majority.*" If so, it would imply that some of the Corinthians had refused to acquiesce in St. Paul's sentence, and had continued in the society of the excommunicated man. But it is probably better to take it as simply meaning the Church as a whole.

*is sufficient*, or "*is a satisfaction.*" That is to say, the punishment already undergone had a satisfactory value; for though the man was excommunicated being impenitent (for if penitent he would never have been excommunicated), and in that state he could not make any satisfaction by his sufferings; yet as he repented when he was excluded from the Church, his separation then acquired a satisfactory value. But it does not mean that his punishment was a complete satisfaction, for the word "*pardon*" means to give out of charity or as a favour something which is not due of justice. But (1) It was sufficient to test the reality and thoroughness of his penitence, and so make indulgence not imprudent; and (2) greater rigour might lead the penitent to desperation, and so cause a worse evil.

7. *you should rather pardon.* St. Paul writes this to the Church of Corinth, which he wishes to exercise this power through its prelates, but with the co-operation of the laity. The fact that he thus takes the Corinthian Church into partnership with himself in granting a pardon, which his apostolic power would have permitted him to grant without their concurrence, does not derogate from his authority, nor is it done without sufficient reason. For we may consider—(1) That he had clearly vindicated his authority by ordering the excommunication (1 Cor. v. 3, 11). (2) He uses his authority also in this place both by his call for obedience (*v.* 9), and by undertaking to ratify their pardon "*in the person of Christ.*" (3) Knowing their distress at what has occurred, he charitably wishes to give them a leading place in the pleasant work of absolution, though he had taken upon himself the disagreeable task of inflicting the excommunication, and had only ordered them to carry that sentence into effect. In this way he hopes to win their greater promptitude in releasing the penitent man. We may notice also that in acting thus there is an analogy between the apostle's

8 with overmuch sorrow. For which cause I beseech you,
9 that you would confirm your charity towards him. For to this end also did I write, that I may know the experiment
10 of you, whether you be obedient in all things. And to

practice and that of his Master; who had said, "Whatsoever you shall bind upon earth, shall be bound also in heaven; and whatsoever you shall loose upon earth, shall be loosed also in heaven"—thus delegating His divine power to his ministers, and promising to ratify their exercise of it; so here St. Paul delegates to his subordinates in turn the exercise of this same power, and promises that he will confirm their pardon by the power which he has received from God.

*overmuch.* St. Paul does not mean that contrition can ever be excessive; but the grief arising from excommunication, from exclusion from the company of Christians, and from the public disgrace incurred, may be so. This excess of sorrow might lead the sinner to lose all hope either of forgiveness, or else of release from his temporal punishments; and might lead him in consequence to abandon himself to vice (cf. Eph. iv. 19).

**8.** *confirm* (κυρῶσαι). The word probably implies a formal decree restoring him to the communion of the Church.

**9.** *that I may know the experiment of you.* This is a Hebrew idiom, and means no more than "*that I might prove.*"

*did I write.* Though this is in the past tense, it is no evidence that St. Paul alludes here to any writing previous to the present Epistle; for it is the Greek idiom to use the past tense in writing letters in reference to what will be past when the letter is read by those to whom it is addressed. Accordingly most commentators consider that it refers to the words immediately preceding, i.e., *that I may prove your obedience in charity now, as I have already had proof of it in severity, when you excommunicated the man at my bidding: thus you will be shown obedient in all things.* But some have supposed that the apostle refers to his first Epistle, and means, *I wrote to you commanding that the man should be excommunicated, feeling sure that if you were obedient in a matter of such difficulty, you would be obedient in anything I had occasion to require of you.*

**10.** *you have pardoned.* The Greek verb is here in the present tense (χαρίζεσθε), though in the following sentence it is in the perfect. It is possible that St. Paul is still referring to the case of pardoning the incestuous man, but it is a more probable supposition that in this verse and the following he is speaking of the granting of such pardons in general. He promises to ratify by his apostolic authority whatever pardons they may find it desirable to grant.

*for your sakes.* The apostle says that whenever he has used that power which he possesses as the representative of Christ to grant a pardon, he has always done so with a view to the interests of the Church: and he puts his conduct forward as an example to be followed whom you have pardoned anything, I also. For what I have pardoned, if I have pardoned anything, for your sakes have I done it in the person of Christ, that we be not over- 11 reached by Satan. For we are not ignorant of his devices.

And when I was come to Troas for the gospel of Christ, 12 by the prelates of the Church (who also bear the person of Christ) in exercising their power of binding and loosing.

*in the person of Christ* (ἐν προσώπῳ χριστοῦ). The word προσωπον means primarily, "*face*," and it is used in this sense in chap. iii. 7, 13. 18; iv. 6; v. 12, and in other passages of the New Testament; but it is never used as meaning "*in the presence of*," which is always represented by another Greek word. This latter rendering was adopted by most of the early Protestant translators of the Bible, and by Calvin, Beza, and Cranmer, who desired to minimise the Divine authority of the clergy: but it is abandoned by modern Protestants, and it is certainly untenable. It may be translated "*face*," but the translation "*person*" is quite in accordance with the Greek, and is otherwise preferable. The meaning is that the apostle is the representative of Christ, so that his acts of binding and loosing are the acts of Christ. If we follow the less probable alternative of translating the word by "*face*," it means that the apostle bore, as it were, the image and appearance of our Lord, in whose name he acted; and thus the meaning is practically unaffected. As he had excommunicated the incestuous man in the name of Christ and by His power (1 Cor. v. 4), so it is also by Christ, whose power and authority he bears, that the apostle, and after him other prelates, grant pardon.

**11.** *overreached.* This word means *to get an unjust advantage over another.* It is particularly appropriate here, for not only is all the power of the devil a usurpation, but when he gains an advantage, not through sin, but through an excessive use of well-meant, though indiscreet, rigour, such an advantage may well be called more than is just.

*we are not ignorant.* St. Paul does not mean to say that he knows all the wiles of Satan, for they are fully known only to God: but that he has such a knowledge of them as suffices for the matter in hand.

*devices*—that is, tricks of cunning and deceit, e.g., persuading to what is evil under the semblance of good. In this way the devil has at various times, under the same specious form, caused the ruin of many souls; and particularly in the heresy of Novatian, and in that of the Jansenists, both of which, by their excessive rigour in dealing with penitent sinners, served the cause of Satan, and not the glory of God.

**12.** *Troas.* The city of Troas, in the district of the same name, is situated on the Eastern side of the Hellespont, and is said to have occupied the site of Troy. St. Paul had visited this place before (Acts xvi. 8), but in consequence of a vision had gone on to Macedonia without making a long stay there. Shortly after the visit here mentioned he spent a week there (Acts xx. 5–12); and it is evident

13 and a door was opened unto me in the Lord, I had no rest in my spirit, because I found not Titus my brother, but bidding them farewell, I went into Macedonia.

14 Now thanks be to God, who always maketh us to triumph in CHRIST JESUS, and manifesteth the odour of his
15 knowledge by us in every place. For we are the good odour of Christ unto God, in them that are saved, and in
16 them that perish. To the one indeed the odour of death

that at that time there were many Christians in the place (cf. also 2 Tim. iv. 13).

*a door was opened unto me in the Lord.* That is, an opportunity was afforded of making converts by our Lord's working, preparing the hearts of the people to accept the Faith.

**13.** *I had no rest in my spirit, because I found not Titus my brother.* We learn from ch. vii., that Titus had been sent to Corinth by St. Paul to obtain news of the condition of the Church there. (See Introduction, Chap. iv.). Hence St. Paul was very anxious to meet him as soon as possible, in order to learn from him whether the Corinthians had amended. Therefore, as he did not find him at Troas, he went forward at once to Macedonia ; and had no rest until he met him, and learned of the reformation that had taken place (vii. 5-7). He introduces this fact here, evidently for the purpose of still further excusing his delay in coming to Corinth, by showing that, though he was absent from them, he was very far from being forgetful of them.

**14.** *triumph.* A Roman triumph was the sequel to a brilliant victory. The victorious general made his entrance into the city at the head of his army, preceded by the prisoners and spoils of war. The idea of a triumph involves, therefore, not merely a victory, but a victory of exceptional brilliance and glory. The Greek word (θριαμβεύοντι) means ordinarily "*to lead in triumph,*" but here it is used in the sense of "*to cause to triumph,*" or "*to make us sharers in his triumph.*" Though St. Paul had undergone many trials and sufferings, yet he regarded the news which he received in Macedonia of the amendment of the Corinthians as more than compensating for them all.

*manifesteth the odour of his knowledge,* that is, *he scatters the knowledge of Himself like a sweet scent in all directions, by means of his apostles* (cf. Cant. i. 2-3). Incense was an invariable accompaniment of a triumph ; and St. Paul, continuing the metaphor, compares himself to the incense-bearer.

**15.** *we are the good odour.* That is to say, *we spread abroad the good odour.* The phrase must be taken in a causal sense (cf. Cant. vi. 1, and also Matt. v. 16).

**16.** *odour of death.* The knowledge of our Lord is a good odour in itself, even though it is the "*odour of death*" to those who refuse to believe, and who receive in consequence a greater condemnation (cf.

unto death; but to the others the odour of life unto life. And for these things who is so sufficient? For we are not as many adulterating the word of God, but with sincerity, but as from God, before God in Christ we speak.

## CHAPTER III.

DO we begin again to commend ourselves? Or do we need (as some do) epistles of commendation to you,

the prophecy of Simeon, Luke ii. 34). Similarly the Church sings of the Blessed Sacrament, "Mors est malis, vita bonis"—"It is death to the guilty, life to the good."

*For these things who is so sufficient?* The word "*so*" corresponds to nothing in the Greek. The meaning is that none is sufficient *of himself* to exercise the apostolate, which is what St. Paul is here speaking of. In his humility he does not attribute to his own powers the success of his ministry, but refers it all to God. At the same time he denies, by implication, the sufficiency of the false apostles, to whom he alludes in the next verse, who have received no such powers from God. He explains this in *vv.* 5, 6 of the following chapter.

17. *adulterating.* The word means "*making merchandise of.*" It therefore means dealing in the word of God for gain or glory, like men who vend their own wares. Such persons commonly strive to make the subject of their preaching pleasant rather than profitable to their hearers, and so readily adulterate the truth. We may compare the Protestants in the sixteenth century, who sought to win acceptance by abolishing the Sacrament of Penance, and denying the necessity of good works in justification; or the more modern heretics who have destroyed the indissolubility of marriage, and are denying the existence of hell.

*as from God*—i.e., as sent from God.

*before God*—i.e., acting as in His presence, and promoting His glory.

*in Christ*—i.e., in the mystical body of Christ which is His Church, and therefore in the person of Christ, as bearing authority given by Him.

## CHAPTER III.

1. *again.* In his first Epistle (esp. chap. ix.) St. Paul seemed to commend himself, and again in the preceding verse he seems to resume this self-commendation. He therefore considers it necessary to say a few words to refute this charge, which, perhaps, had actually been brought forward by his opponents. This he does, by showing, first (*vv.* 2, 3), that such conduct would be quite superfluous, and secondly (*vv.* 5, 6), that any praise of his own office is to be ascribed, not to himself, but to God, who conferred the apostolic powers upon him.

*epistles of commendation.* It is evident from this verse that such

² or from you? You are our epistle, written in our hearts,
³ which is known and read by all men: being manifested, that you are the epistle of Christ, ministered by us, and written not with ink, but with the spirit of the living God: not in tables of stone, but in the fleshy tables of the heart.

letters were already in use in apostolic times. They were used in the case of laymen, who had occasion to travel from their homes, and that in order to secure them a reception and admission to Holy Communion in other Churches; and also for the clergy, as evidence of their ordination and orthodoxy, so as to prevent any unauthorized persons being admitted to say Mass before the faithful. St. Paul had no need of such letters *to* the Corinthians, who knew him well; nor yet *from* the Corinthians, since the work he had done amongst them gave him sufficient notoriety wherever Corinth was known.

2. *you are our epistle;* that is, *you are yourselves the letter commending us.*

*written in our hearts:* so that he carries this epistle with him everywhere and exhibits it for his commendation. His love for the Corinthians caused them to be always imprinted on his heart: as our Lord says to His Church: "I will not forget thee. Behold I have graven thee in My hands; thy walls are always before my eyes" (Isa. xlix. 15, 16).

*known and read by all men:* because the ame of the Corinthians was wide-spread, and while the pagan city of Corinth was a place of notorious profligacy and vice, the contrast to this presented by the Christian Church there, in spite of some evil members, was most striking.

3. *the epistle of Christ.* This is taken by some to mean that the law of Christ was preserved among them, so that they were, as it were, an Epistle containing the law of Christ. But it is simpler, and suits the context better, to understand it as meaning an Epistle of which Christ is the author, because their conversion was by his power.

*ministered by us*—i.e., *written by our ministry.*

*the living God.* St. Paul puts in the word "living," not only because God lives, but also because He is the source of all life, both natural and supernatural.

*not in tables of stone.* The sequel shows that there is an allusion here to the law of Moses, which was written on stone tablets, with which is contrasted the law of the New Testament, written by the Holy Ghost on hearts softened by grace and made ready to obey. (Cf. Ezech. xxxvi. 26-28, "I will take away the stony heart out of your flesh, and will give you a heart of flesh. And I will put my spirit in the midst of you; and I will cause you to walk in my commandments, and to keep my judgments, and do them . . . and you shall be my people, and I will be your God." Cf. also Ezech. xi. 19, 20; Jer. xxxi. 31-33).

And such confidence we have, through Christ, towards God. 1 Not that we are sufficient to think anything of ourselves, as 5 of ourselves; but our sufficiency is from God, who also 6 hath made us fit ministers of the new testament, not in the letter, but in the spirit. For the letter killeth: but the spirit quickeneth.

**4.** *such confidence we have through Christ.* That is to say, *we have the confidence, through the grace of Christ, that you are our Epistle* (the evidence of our Divine mission).

*towards God,* or "*in God's presence.*" This means a confidence which he is not ashamed to exhibit before God, because, though he glories in the excellence of his ministry, he does not take the credit of it to himself.

**5.** *not that we are sufficient.* . . . These words have been interpreted in two different ways. (1) *We are not able by our own natural powers without the co-operation of grace, even to think a good thought by ourselves—much more then is it due to God's grace that we are made sufficient to perform the ministry of the New Testament.* This interpretation was followed by St. Augustine, who proved from it, against the Semipelagian heresy, that the beginning of faith and of good works must come from the grace of the Holy Ghost, which first rouses the will to make a beginning, and then strengthens it and works with it. Calvin, indeed, argues from this passage that the will has no power, but that all good works are due entirely to grace, without any co-operation of freewill at all; but this sense the words will not support, for St. Paul denies the sufficiency, not the reality, of free-will. (2) But a more probable and better supported interpretation is to take the word λογίσασθαι ("*think*") as "*reckon*" or "*account,*" a meaning which it naturally bears. Then the passage will mean; *We are not in ourselves of sufficient worth to reckon any of our own good works as wrought by our own power.* We might expect the apostle to say: *We are not sufficient to do anything good by our own power*—but his humility makes him go further and say, in effect, *We are so worthless in ourselves that we not only can do nothing, but that it is impossible for us even to profess to do anything, by our own strength, but all our power to do good is derived from God, who (in addition to his other graces) has also given us these graces necessary for the exercise of the apostolate.* This explanation agrees with the context better than the former, because the question evidently is of exercising the apostolic functions, not of having good thoughts.

**6.** *the new testament.* This of course does not mean the book known by that name, but the Gospel dispensation, under the fulness of grace and truth revealed and given by our Lord.

*not in the letter, but in the spirit.* By this phrase St. Paul contrasts the old dispensation with the new. It corresponds to what he has said in *v.* 2. The old dispensation consisted principally in positive

7 Now if the ministration of death, engraven with letters upon stones, was glorious: so that the children of Israel could not steadfastly behold the face of Moses, for the
8 glory of his countenance, which is made void: how shall

enactments, such as the Ten Commandments; but the new dispensation is not so much concerned with giving fresh precepts, as in bringing to men the assistance of the Holy Ghost, who gives them grace and enables them to fulfil the commandments, which in their own power they could not do. So St. John says "The law was given by Moses, grace and truth came by JESUS CHRIST" (John i. 17).

*the letter killeth, but the spirit quickeneth.* See Appendix IV.

**7, 8.** In these verses the apostle shows that the ministry of the New Testament excels that of the Old in three respects:

(1) *In its effect*, namely, life or death.

(2) *In the manner of its preservation.* The Old Law was handed down engraven in letters on stone tablets; but the New Law is impressed by the Holy Ghost upon the hearts of men, and is preserved, not merely in written documents, but in the tradition of the Living Church, inspired by the Holy Ghost.

(3) *In perfection.* The glory of the Old Law was as transitory as the glory upon the face of Moses, but the New brings with it the hope of eternal glory (cf. iv. 17).

**7.** *the face of Moses.* When God gave the Law to Moses upon Sinai, the latter remained forty days upon the mountain fasting, and was allowed to see a part of God's glory (Exod. xxxiii. 22, 23; xxxiv. 28); not indeed the uncreated and essential Glory of God, but a certain created manifestation of the same. This glory of God was the same as that which rested upon the tabernacle, and which preceded the Israelites in their march through the desert. It is called in Hebrew the Shechinah. Cf. Exod. xiii. 21, 22; xiv. 19, 20; xxv. 8; xl. 31-36; 3 Kings viii. 10, 11, &c. When Moses came down again to the people, rays of light shone from his face, being, as it were, a reflection of the Glory of God, in whose presence he had been, and designed by God both as an honour to His prophet, and to attest the Divine origin of that Law which Moses had to deliver to the people. But inasmuch as this Law was itself temporary, and was to last only until the coming of Christ, this transitoriness also was typified by the fact that the glory which shone from the face of Moses was not permanent, but only lasted a short time after his converse with God (Exod. xxxiv. 29-35). In the next chapter (*v.* 6) we shall see how St. Paul contrasts this evanescent brightness with the light which shines perpetually from the Divine Face of our Lord.

*could not steadfastly behold.* The Israelites were not yet prepared to behold the full glory which God had to reveal; and this was typified by the fact that they were afraid when they saw the glory upon the face of Moses.

*which is made void:* rather "*which was transient.*" As the glory

not the ministration of the Spirit be rather in glory? For 9
if the ministration of condemnation be glory, much more
the ministration of justice aboundeth in glory. For even 10
that which was glorious in this part was not glorified, by
reason of the glory that excelleth. For if that which is 11
done away was glorious, much more that which remaineth
is in glory.

Having therefore such hope, we use much confidence: 12
And not as Moses put a veil upon his face that the 13
children of Israel might not steadfastly look on the face

on the face of Moses was passing away even while he was speaking to
the people; so that which was symbolized by it, the glory of the Old
Dispensation, was intended to be only temporary.

**9.** *if the ministration of condemnation be glory*. . . . The law had
no power to justify men: therefore it must give less glory to its ministers than the Gospel, which justifies by giving inward life through the
operation of the Holy Ghost.

**10, 11.** In these verses St. Paul meets a possible objection of his
opponents, who might indeed acknowledge that the New Testament
was better than the Old, and yet insist that the Old Testament had
a glory of its own which was not to be rejected. He therefore adds
that the glory of the Law, great as it might be in itself, was, by comparison with the Gospel, nothing at all.

**10.** *even that which was glorious*. . . . The passage may be better
translated "*That which was glorified, was not glorified in this respect, by
reason of the glory which excelleth*": that is to say that, glorious as it
truly was, it had no glory in comparison with the ministry of the Gospel;
just as a lantern may be considered as giving a bright light in the night,
but when the sun rises it has, by comparison, no brightness at all, so
that no one would suppose that, by reason of the light it gave, the
lantern should be still left burning.

**11.** *that which is done away*, or rather "*which is transient.*"
*that which remaineth*, or, "*which is permanent.*"

**12–18.** St. Paul having compared the glory of the Old Testament
Ministry with that of the New in its effect (*vv.* 6, 9), in the manner of
its preservation (*vv.* 7, 8), and in its permanence (*vv.* 7, 11), now proceeds to make a comparison between the clearness and completeness of
the two revelations (*vv.* 12–16), and to show the consequence of the
superiority of the Gospel (*vv.* 17, 18).

**12.** *such hope*, that is the hope, (founded on the permanence of the
glory of the New Testament, which he administered) that by a faithful
ministry he may be admitted to enjoy that glory for ever.
*confidence* (παρρησία), that is, "*plain-speaking.*"

**13.** *the face of that which is made void.* Another reading, which is
more probable, puts "*end*" instead of "*face.*" "*Which is made void,*"

14 of that which is made void. But their senses were made dull. For until this present day, the self-same veil, in the reading of the old testament, remaineth not taken away 15 (because in Christ it is made void). But even until this day when Moses is read, the veil is upon their heart. 16 But when they shall be converted to the Lord, the veil

would be better translated as in *v.* 7, "*which was transient.*" Some commentators suppose that by "*the end of that which was transient*" is meant the ending of the transient glory. According to this view Moses put the veil before his face that the people might not see the brightness passing away, because it was not his wish to teach them that the glory of the Law would have an end. The transitoriness of the Law was indeed revealed to the Israelites, but this was done gradually through the prophets. If it had been made known at the beginning, it might only have had the result of destroying the people's respect for the Law. The apostles of the New Testament have no need of such reserve, but can speak plainly, because the glory of the New Testament is not transient. But a better interpretation, and one more in accordance both with the context and with the use of the word τέλος (end) by St. Paul, is to suppose it to mean the *object* or *scope* of the law, namely Christ (cf. Rom. x. 4). Therefore God inspired Moses to veil his face, in order to signify that when the Law was given, something still remained hidden, until Christ came to tear away the veil (cf. *v.* 14).

**14-16.** In these verses we see that the use of the veil as a symbol is somewhat changed. A veil can hide an object, either by being placed over the object itself (as it was placed over the face of Moses); or by being put before the eyes of the persons who are thus prevented from seeing. In the former sense, when our Lord, who is the Truth, came into the world, the veil was removed. The glory of God was no longer veiled under types, but was perfectly revealed to the Church; and as a symbol of this, at the moment when our Lord, by His death, brought the old dispensation to an end, the veil of the Temple (hiding the visible Glory of God in the Holy of Holies), was rent in two. But while there was now no veil before the revelation of God, those Jews who lacked the gift of Faith still had one before the eyes of their souls; and were not able to see that in Christ the veil had been removed from the previous partial revelation of God (cf. John ix. 39-41).

**14.** *the old testament.* This is the only place where this phrase is used in Scripture to express writings. It does not here mean all those books which we include under that name, (as is evident from the following verse), but only the books of Moses in which the Law was contained.

**16.** *when they shall be converted to the Lord.* . . . St. Paul is still using the same figure as before. When Moses went into God's presence, he removed the veil, and saw the glory of God. In a similar way St.

shall be taken away. Now the Lord is a Spirit. And 17 where the Spirit of the Lord is, there is liberty. But we 18 all, beholding the glory of the Lord with open face, are

Paul says that when the Israelites, or any of them, turn to God, the veil shall be removed from their faces.

**17.** *a Spirit.* τὸ πνεῦμα, that is, "*the Spirit.*" Still continuing the same comparison. St. Paul, who has said in the previous verse that the Jews must turn to the Lord as Moses did, now goes on to explain that the Lord to whom they must turn is the Spirit, that is the Holy Ghost, who operates in the New Testament (as he has already explained in *vv.* 3 and 6). The verse thus contains an assertion of the Divinity of the Holy Ghost.

*the Spirit of the Lord.* The Holy Ghost is not only Himself God, but is also the "Spirit of God," since He proceeds from the other Two Persons of the Blessed Trinity.

*liberty.* The meaning of this is explained at length by St. Paul in various passages of his Epistles (cf. especially Gal. iv. 1-7; v. 13-26). It was prophesied by Isaias (cf. Isa. xlii. 6, 7, lxi. i). The freedom of the New Testament is a freedom of the understanding, which receives a full knowledge of the Truth without symbols and veils, and a liberty of the will which gains grace to serve God from love of justice, and not merely from fear of punishment. It was an error of some early heretics, (cf. 2 Peter ii. 19) which was revived in the sixteenth century by the Anabaptists, that spiritual men were not bound to obey the precepts of the Divine Law. This arose from a false idea of liberty; for the man who commits sin is not free, but is the slave of sin (cf. John viii. 34; Rom. vi. 15-23, see also 1 Peter ii. 16).

**18.** *beholding;* Greek κατοπτριζόμενοι, that is either "*seeing as in a mirror,*" or "*reflecting as in a mirror,*" but the latter meaning suits the context better. In this verse St. Paul shows how the veil is altogether taken away from all converts to the Faith.

*with open face:* that is "*with unveiled face.*" As Moses entered into the presence of God with his face uncovered, and in consequence reflected from his own face some of the glory manifested to him; so now the souls of all the faithful can behold unveiled, and reflect, the glory of God Himself, which shines upon them from the Divine Face of our Blessed Lord, which is itself the perfect Image of the Divine glory (iv. *v.* 6). If we accept the translation "*beholding in a mirror,*" then the "*mirror*" is itself the Face of our Lord, and the "*glory*" is the revelation made through Him; but this does not suit the context so well, for we are "*transformed into the image*" of God's glory, not so much by looking at it as it exists in our Lord, but rather by having it marked or impressed upon us, as the image is marked on the mirror. For the Divine Image is marked upon the human soul by the operation of the Holy Ghost, both in the Sacraments and in the other workings of grace; so that the faithful, in proportion as they correspond with grace become more and more "partakers of the Divine transformed into the same image from glory to glory, as by the Spirit of the Lord.

## CHAPTER IV.

THEREFORE seeing we have *this* ministration, according as we have obtained mercy, we faint not. 2 But we renounce the hidden things of dishonesty, not walking in craftiness, nor adulterating the word of God,

nature" (2 Peter i. 4), and transformed into God. And this transformation, though it can never be complete upon earth, is perfected in the saints in heaven (cf. 1 John iii. 2).

*transformed.* This is the same word which is used of the transfiguration of our Lord (Matt. xvii. 2; Mark ix. 1).

*from glory to glory:* that is to say, from one degree of glory to another. St. Thomas distinguishes three grades of progress: (1) from the glory of that knowledge of God which is by nature to that which is by faith; (2) from the glory of the knowledge of the Old Testament, to that of the knowledge of the grace of the New Testament; (3) from all of these to the glory of the Beatific Vision (cf. 1 Cor. xiii. 12).

### CHAPTER IV.

In this chapter St. Paul continues his praise of the ministry of the gospel: and having shown how excellent it is in itself, he proceeds to speak of his employment of it, both in his preaching (vv. 1-6), and in his patient endurance of suffering, which he accepts and offers for their sakes (vv. 7-15).

1. *this ministry*— i.e., a ministry of such dignity as he has described it to be.

*according as* . . . This belongs to what precedes. He has this ministration, not as from himself, but according to the mercy he has received from God. The apostle explains this more fully in 1 Tim. i. 12-16, where he says that God's mercy was shown both in his conversion and in his being called to the apostolate for the sake of the increase of the Church by his means.

*we faint not.* St. Paul is here resuming what he said in chap. iii. 12: *We speak plainly and boldly, and do not shrink back through weakness or cowardice from any difficulties,* such as are mentioned in vv. 8, &c.

2. This verse contains a threefold antithesis: (1) *We renounce the hidden things of dishonesty* . . . *commending ourselves to every man's conscience;* (2) *not walking in craftiness* . . . (but) *in the sight of God;* (3) *not adulterating the Word of God, but manifesting the truth.*

*the hidden things of dishonesty.* Dishonesty here means *what is dis-*

but by manifestation of the truth commending ourselves to
every man's conscience, in the sight of God.  And if our 3
gospel be also hid ; it is hid to them that are lost, in whom 4
the god of this world hath blinded the minds of unbelievers,

*honourable;* such sins as men hide, and do not wish to have known even to their fellowmen, much less to God (cf. John iii. 19-21). St. Paul teaches us here that all sin is a hindrance both to those who are seeking the light of truth, and to those who would declare it to others.

*not walking in craftiness*—that is *hypocrisy*, or *dissimulation*. St. Paul implies that he has rejected not only evil works, but also evil intention.

*adulterating.* This means, as in chap. ii. 17, either mixing false doctrine with the true, or preaching to obtain glory or gain.

*commending ourselves,* i.e., not by speaking good about himself, which might very well not be believed, but by doing good.

*to every man's conscience.* St. Paul said in his First Epistle to the Corinthians, " I became all things to all men that I might save all " (cf. 1 Cor. ix. 19-22). He implies here that when the gospel is clearly preached it is commended to every man's conscience, so that those who do not receive it are resisting their consciences.

3-6.  In these verses St. Paul shows that if any do not receive this gospel, it is not because of any fault of the gospel, but of a blindness on the part of the unbelievers, which is, (ordinarily at least) the result of sin : since his gospel is no other than the gospel of Christ, which derives its power of illuminating from God Himself, the Author of all light.

*hid.* The word means "*veiled,*" and is an allusion to the similitude of the previous chapter.

*that are lost.* This should be translated, "*who are perishing*" (ἐν τοῖς ἀπολλυμένοις, Vulg. " in iis, qui pereunt ").

4.  *the god of this world.* Many ancient commentators suppose that by this is meant God Himself, who created and sustains this world ; and who may be said to blind the minds of unbelievers, inasmuch as He withdraws His grace from those who are obstinate in refusing to believe. In support of this is the fact that God alone, in the strictest sense, is God of this world ; but nevertheless it appears better to understand it as meaning the devil, who may be called the god of this world—(1) because he is permitted to exercise a certain power in this world by tempting men (cf. Apoc. xii. 12) ; (2) because there are so many in this world who follow him as if he were their god, that is, as though he had a claim to their service, and over whom he exercises dominion ; (3) he is god of this world in the sense in which the "*world*" is often used by our Lord and His apostles to denote the whole body of men who act without any regard to God as their last end, and who are opposed to the Church.  It is in this sense that the devil himself in tempting our Lord claimed power over all the kingdoms of the world ; with great presumption indeed, yet at least acknowledging that he did

that the light of the gospel of the glory of Christ, who is
5 the image of God, should not shine unto them. For we
preach not ourselves, but JESUS CHRIST our Lord: and
6 ourselves your servants through JESUS. For God, who
commanded the light to shine out of darkness, hath shined

not have this power of himself, but only as it was delivered to him (Luke iv. 6). Our Lord also three times called the devil the "prince of this world," and declared that by the power of His crucifixion the usurped power of the devil should be overthrown (John xii. 31; also xiv. 30; xvi. 11).

*hath blinded*, i.e., by suggesting and inclining them to sin, which renders them less able to see the truth.

*light* (τὸν φωτισμόν, Vulg. illuminatio). It would be better translated "*illumination*" or "*enlightenment*." God the Father is the original source of all light (1 John i. 5), and from this original light is derived its image, God the Son; who in the Nicene Creed is called "light from light" (lumen de lumine); and in the Epistle to the Hebrews is called the "brightness of the Father's glory and the figure of His substance" (Heb. i. 3). The Son having become incarnate, manifested to men the brightness of God (John i. 9, 14; viii. 12) by His Divine working. The gospel declares the glory of Christ, which is the glory of God, since Christ is the *perfect* image of God, being (unlike other imperfect images) in all things equal to Him Whose image He is. This declaration has a power of enlightening, by the help of grace, those who are not hindered by sin from receiving it.

5. *ourselves your servants through* JESUS. That is to say, he did not commend himself, but made himself the servant of the Church, existing only for their spiritual welfare (cf. 1 Cor. ix. 19).

6. *God, who commanded.* . . . St. Paul, having spoken of his own ministry at the end of the last verse, now sums up this section of his Epistle. He says that God who, by His mere fiat, brought light out of darkness, has shone in his heart (namely, at his conversion, Acts ix. 3), and not only shines upon and in him, but also shines forth from him to the enlightening of others, by giving them a knowledge of the glory of God, a glory which shines on the face of CHRIST JESUS.

*hath shined in our hearts.* As the created manifestation of God's glory enlightened the face of Moses, and being reflected therefrom, illuminated also the children of Israel; in the same manner, but in a far higher degree, the perfect and uncreated glory of God, made manifest in our Lord's sacred humanity, shines upon the apostles and priests of the New Testament, and being reflected from them enlightens both those who believe through their ministry, and also the whole Church of God. The antithesis is between the glory illuminating the face of Moses, and that illuminating the apostles. It is not directly between Moses and our Lord. But as the latter glory has its most perfect manifestation in our Blessed Lord, and as moreover the apostles, only as members of Christ, either have light themselves, or give it to others, therefore St.

in our hearts, to give the light of the knowledge of the glory of God in the face of CHRIST JESUS.

But we have this treasure in earthen vessels, that the excellency may be of the power of God, and not of us. In all things we suffer tribulation, but are not distressed: we are straitened, but are not destitute: we suffer persecution, but are not forsaken: we are cast down, but we perish not: always bearing about in our body the 7 8 9 10

Paul speaks of the enlightenment which shines from himself, as existing in the Divine Face of our Lord.

**7-15.** In this passage St. Paul begins to declare the greatness of his ministry in another way. He has shown how great a dignity it is to have the glory of the apostleship; he now proceeds to rejoice that he is made a partner with our Lord, not only in His glory, but also in His suffering; without which suffering that glory would be imperfect, because it would not be sure to be attributed solely to God. See *vv.* 7, 15.

**7.** *treasure*: that is, the light with which he enlightens others.

*in earthen vessels* has been explained in two ways: either (1) our bodies, which are formed of the dust of the ground (Gen. ii. 7; iii. 19); or (2) our whole persons, as being weak and unworthy of such dignity; as Isaias says (lxiv. 8), "Thou art our Father, and we are clay."

**8, 9.** God wishes His apostle to be despised and persecuted, in order that it may be quite evident that the power of the ministry is derived only from God, and not from St. Paul himself.

The four clauses in these two verses probably correspond to no exact distinction of different modes of suffering.

**8** *not distressed*. The word expresses the situation of a man who is in a difficulty which offers no way of escape. It implies that while those who trust only in the world have no remedy if they are in tribulation from the world, those who trust in God are never left without resource. For if the world afflicts them, they still have a means of escape by God's help.

*straitened, but not destitute.* This would be better translated "*in want, but not in absolute want*."

**9.** *cast down*, or rather "*struck down*," i.e., to the danger of death.

**10 12.** St. Paul accepts all his sufferings not only with patience, but with eagerness: because he recognizes in them an opportunity of meriting, and a pledge of receiving, future glory with our Lord; and because he wishes to offer them for the salvation of his converts.

*mortification.* That is "*putting to death*." It includes both the actual renunciation of all sin, as he said in writing to the Romans, "Reckon that you are dead to sin, but alive unto God" (Rom. vi. 11); and more especially the patient endurance of the sufferings which he continually had to undergo, and through which he hoped to obtain a share in our Lord's resurrection (cf. Phil. iii. 8-12). See note on i. 5.

mortification of JESUS, that the life also of JESUS may be made manifest in our bodies. For we who live are always delivered unto death for JESUS' sake: that the life also of JESUS may be made manifest in our mortal flesh. So then death worketh in us, but life in you. But having the same spirit of faith, as it is written: *I believed, for which cause I have spoken:* we also believe, for which cause we speak also: knowing that he who raised up JESUS will raise up us also with JESUS, and place us with you. For all things *are* for your sakes: that the grace abounding through many may abound in thanksgiving unto the glory of God.

*made manifest.* This is chiefly the case in the resurrection of our bodies, which are made to live with the life of our Lord, even as He said, "Because I live, ye shall live also."

**11.** *we who live,* i.e., *as long as our life on earth lasts.*

*are always delivered unto death;* that is, "*are always being delivered.*" St. Paul's life was perpetual martyrdom; as the Psalmist says, "For thy sake we are killed all the day long" (Ps. xliii. 22); or as St. Paul said himself, "I die daily" (1 Cor. xv. 31). This martyrdom is quite apart from the actual danger of death, in which St. Paul has often found himself (cf. i. 8, 9; Acts xiv. 18, &c.).

**12.** *death worketh in us, but life in you;* that is, *sufferings of mind and body, equivalent to death, continually have dominion over me. Though you do not indeed share these sufferings, yet by virtue of them* (which I offer for your welfare) *you are made partakers of the spiritual life to which they lead.*

**13, 14.** St. Paul shows that the power to endure his sufferings rests only upon the certainty of faith, infused into his heart by the Holy Ghost, and assuring him of eternal life in our Lord.

**13.** *the same,* that is, the same as that of the Psalmist; for though the *object* of faith has become more fully manifested, yet the Spirit and the faith are the same.

*spirit.* It is not clear whether by this word we are to understand the Holy Ghost, who imparts the faith, or the quality or virtue of faith itself, which is imparted.

*I believed.* (Ps. cxv. 10.) The saints of the Old Testament had divine faith, and confessed their faith (cf. Heb. xi.).

**14.** *knowing,* that is, with the certainty of faith, for divine faith is the most certain form of knowledge.

*with* JESUS, that is, to receive the same glory as our Lord. The living members cannot be separated from their Head, who has said, "Where I am, there also shall my minister be" (John xii. 26).

**15.** *all things are for your sakes.* These words explain the last clause of the preceding verse. He can well couple them with himself, because he does and suffers all things for their good.

For which cause we faint not: but though our outward 16 man is corrupted, yet the inward man is renewed day by day. For that which is at present momentary and light of 17 our tribulation, worketh for us above measure exceedingly an eternal weight of glory; while we look not at the things 18

*that the grace abounding through many.* . . . This clause probably means, "*that the grace having abounded by means of many may cause the thanksgiving to abound unto the glory of God.*"

*through many.* St. Paul, having said that all his sufferings were endured for their sakes, does not wish to seem to assume to himself all the merit for the grace they had received, and therefore he adds these words, implying that the prayers of all the members of the Corinthian Church had had a share in obtaining grace for them. Some commentators, however, take these words with "*the thanksgiving,*" thus: "*that the abundant grace may cause thanksgiving to abound through many:*" that is to say, that all who receive the grace may join in giving thanks for it.

**16-18.** In these verses St. Paul shows how he is sustained in all sufferings by the fact that things which seem to the body burdensome, are to the soul of him who looks to the purpose of his creation a real source of strength and consolation.

**16.** *for which cause,* namely, because he has an assurance of the resurrection.

*we faint not,* that is, he shrinks from no tribulations, and does not allow them to prevent him from exercising his ministry with confidence (cf. *v.* 1).

*our outward man . . . inward man.* That is called the "*man*" which is the chief part of man. Those who regard only the things of sense and of earth, look on the body and its senses as constituting the chief part of man's nature; but spiritual men, who do not look only upon the surface, but regard things as they really are, look upon the soul as the chief part of man, as in truth it is; and therefore this is called the inward man, and the other the outward man.

*is corrupted,* or rather, "*is being corrupted,*" by constant afflictions and mortifications; by which, on the one hand, the body is brought nearer to the dissolution of death, and on the other hand, when they are endured with patience, the tendency to sin which is in the outward man is destroyed.

*is renewed.* Since the fall, all things tend with age to dissolution. But the supernatural life of the soul is continually renewed by fresh graces; and the patient endurance of sufferings obtains from God many such graces, by which the life of the soul is constantly being renewed and increased by the destruction of sin and error.

**17, 18.** Those who consider the glory cannot be troubled by the tribulations, which are nothing by comparison.

**17.** This verse contains a threefold antithesis. (1) *momentary . . . eternal;* (2) *light . . . weight;* (3) *of affliction . . . of glory.*

which are seen, but at the things which are not seen. For the things which are seen are temporal: but the things which are not seen are eternal.

## CHAPTER V.

FOR we know, if our earthly house of this habitation be dissolved, that we have a building of God, a house

*at present.* There is nothing corresponding to this in the Greek, but it is implied in the word "*momentary.*"
*light.* There is here an apparent contradiction to what was said in i. 8, where St. Paul spoke of his tribulation as burdening him beyond his strength. But that which is burdensome to the body, is light to the spirit inflamed with charity and fortified by the hope of future glory.
**18.** *temporal;* that is, "*temporary.*"

### CHAPTER V.

**1-8.** In these verses St. Paul continues what he has been saying about the resurrection and eternal glory. He expresses his very great desire to enjoy the presence of God, which desire overcomes the natural repugnance to death which he feels. The connection of this passage with the argument of the two preceding chapters is that the apostle of the New Testament will not spare himself any labours or sufferings in the execution of his ministry, knowing that even if the sufferings cause his death, death itself is but the passage to eternal life, or return home after exile.

**1.** *house,* i.e., our earthly body.
*habitation.* The Greek word means a tent, and so it denotes that our life on earth is in its nature temporary, and like that of soldiers or pilgrims marching towards their native land (cf. 2 Pet. i. 13, 14).
*be dissolved,* i.e., by death.
*we have,* that is to say, *we are sure of having.* The present is used for the future to express the certainty of hope.
*a building of God,* namely, the glorified body of the Resurrection.
*of God,* that is, *prepared by God.*
*not made with hands.* Our earthly bodies are not indeed made with hands, but they partake of the nature of all human works in being liable to corruption.
The explanation of this verse contained in the preceding notes is that adopted by most commentators; but there are some who think the reference must be to the glory into which the souls of the saints enter immediately after death, both because the word ἔχομεν, "*we have,*" is in the present tense (i.e., *we have immediately*), and because they suppose St. Paul's argument to be that he is ready to endure sufferings, because if they hasten his death, they only bring him *more speedily* to

not made with hands, eternal in heaven. For in this also we groan, desiring to be clothed upon with our habitation that is from heaven: yet so, that we be found clothed, not naked. For we also, who are in this tabernacle, do groan being burthened: because we would not be unclothed, but clothed upon, that that which is mortal may be swallowed up by life. Now he that maketh us for this very thing is God, who hath given us the pledge of the Spirit. There-

the glory for which he hopes. But this explanation does not agree well with the metaphor of a building, nor with the following verses, and it is rejected by most commentators.

**2-4.** To understand these verses properly, it must be remembered that St. Paul always treats of the end of the world as though it might come during his own life (cf. 1 Thes. iv. 14-16); though he is careful to avoid saying positively that it will come soon (cf. 2 Thess. ii. 1, 2). In these verses St. Paul expresses his desire that our Lord's second coming might be during his own lifetime, not merely because of a natural shrinking from death, but also because he wished to see the consummation of God's kingdom (cf. Apoc. vi. 10).

**2.** *we groan* (cf. Rom. viii. 22-24). These words express the fervent desire of St. Paul to be delivered from his mortal body, with the constant liability to temptation and danger of falling into sin which is attached to it.

*to be clothed upon*, that is, to receive the glorified body without death, as the next verse explains. St. Paul passes from the metaphor of a house or tent to that of clothes—but both represent the body.

**3.** *yet so that we be found.* . . . The meaning is: *we desire to receive our habitation from heaven* (that is, the glorification of the flesh), *while we are still clothed* (in this mortal body), *not naked* (by the separation of the soul from the body in death). Some commentators have supposed that *to be clothed* here meant *clothed with good works* (as in Col. iii. 20); but this meaning does not suit the context of this passage.

**5.** *he that maketh us for this very thing is God.* Our desire of eternal glory is not merely selfish, as some might say, but it is the end for which God has made us, and of which He has assured us by the Holy Ghost infusing into our minds the supernatural virtue of hope.

*the pledge of the Spirit.* See i. 22.

**6-8.** In these verses St. Paul protests that in spite of his natural shrinking from death, and his desire that our Lord's second coming should be in his own life, yet he is ready and willing rather to die than to delay his entry into God's presence.

*absent from the Lord.* The word ἐκδημοῦμεν, translated "*absent*" here, means "*to be on a pilgrimage*," or "*in exile*," away from our home. It is therefore a continuation of the metaphor used in *v.* 1, in which our mortal body is called a tent (cf. Ps. cxix. 5, 6). In the same way

fore having always confidence, knowing that, while we are
7 in the body, we are absent from the Lord. (For we walk
8 by faith and not by sight.) But we are confident, and
have a good will to be absent rather from the body, and
to be present with the Lord.

9 And therefore we labour, whether absent or present, to
10 please him. For we must all be manifested before the
judgment-seat of Christ, that every one may receive the
proper things of the body, according as he hath done,
whether it be good or evil.

the word ἐνδημοῦντες, translated here by "*we are in the body*" and in the following verses by "*to be present*," means "*to be at home*," so that the apostle's meaning is that as long as our mortal body forms our temporary lodging, we are exiles from our true home, which is the presence of our Lord.

*the Lord*, that is, as usually in St. Paul, not the Blessed Trinity, nor God the Father, but the Incarnate Son, our Lord JESUS CHRIST.

**7.** *we walk by faith, and not by sight.* The last verse taken alone might have seemed to deny both that we are always in God's presence even while on earth, and also that our Lord is really bodily present in our midst in the Blessed Sacrament. To avoid any misunderstanding he adds this verse, which explains in what sense the preceding is to be taken. The light of Faith is indeed an illumination of the Holy Ghost, who is really present with us, and directs our steps in our pilgrimage towards our true home. But it is not the perfect enjoyment of our Lord's presence, in which no such light is required, because God is Himself the Light of it (Apoc. xxii. 5), and we shall then see Him face to face whom we now see veiled beneath the Sacramental species (1 Cor. xiii. 12).

**8.** *we are confident.* . . . In this verse St. Paul expresses his desire to complete his pilgrimage, and shows himself triumphant over the shrinking of nature from death. But he does not cease to resign himself in this entirely to God's will, and so he says, in the next verse, "*whether absent or present*." Cf. Phil. i. 23, 24.

**9-17.** St. Paul explains here what means the hope of eternal glory and the certainty of judgment lead him to take in preparation for them while he remains on earth. These are to do always what is most pleasing to God (*v.* 9), and in particular to glorify Him by seeking in all things the profit of his neighbour (*vv.* 11-15), and by ridding himself of all affections that might draw him in the least degree from the service of God (*vv.* 15-17).

*we labour.* Greek φιλοτιμούμεθα, "*we make it our aim*," that is to say, we always keep before our minds the fact that the end of our creation was that we might do that which is pleasing to God.

**10.** *the proper things of the body*, that is, *what we have done while living in the body.*

Knowing therefore the fear of the Lord, we use per- 11
suasion to men: but to God we are manifest. And I
trust also that in your consciences we are manifest. We 12
commend not ourselves again to you, but give you occasion
to glory in our behalf: that you may have *somewhat to
answer* them who glory in face, and not in heart. For 13

*according as*. This does not mean that the rewards of heaven do not exceed the merits of our works, but that they are proportioned to them, so that those who do best in this world receive the highest degree of glory, and *vice versâ*. The judgment referred to in this verse is evidently the particular judgment immediately after death.

**11.** *knowing therefore the fear of the Lord*. . . . The consideration of the holy fear of our Lord JESUS CHRIST leads him to persuade men to fear and to believe. And he establishes his sincerity in so doing by appealing to a twofold testimony: first, that of God, who sees the intentions of his heart; secondly, that of the consciences of his converts (cf. iv. 2).

**12.** *but give you occasion to glory in our behalf*. Lest he should seem to be speaking too much in his own praise, he adds that, if he speaks highly of his own apostolic work, it is for their good, to give them matter for true glorying against their false teachers, who denied that St. Paul possessed any true apostolate.

*in face, and not in heart*, that is, *in outward appearance*, like hypocrites, *and not in inward sincerity*, like the apostle (i. 12). Other commentators explain this to mean *in the outward profession, and the boast that they followed the doctrine of the apostles and had been taught by them, while in fact they were seeking to destroy this doctrine*.

**13.** *whether we be transported in mind, it is to God*. . . Whether he is transported in mind or sober, in either case there is an occasion for his followers to glory in being his disciples; because in the one case it is for the honour of God; in the other for the profit of men.

*transported in mind:* that is, *whether we are mad*. It may mean *whether we act as madmen in praising ourselves and our ministry, we do not do so for our own glory, but for that of God*, because God's honour suffers when the dignity of His servants is not recognized. This would correspond to what he says in xi. 21, 23, and would be explained by the words of iv. 7. Or it may mean, *whether the fervour and zeal of our preaching causes us to be regarded as madmen or fanatics, we are content to be regarded as such in the service of God*. Festus (Acts xxvi. 24, 25) looked on St. Paul as mad, because when he was on trial for his life he was not so anxious to save himself as to convert his judges; and our Lord Himself was called mad for a similar reason (Mark iii. 21, where the Greek word is the same as that used here).

*whether we be sober* is similarly explained in different ways. It means either, *if we speak modestly of ourselves, it is to give you an example;* or, *if we take care by moderate language to avoid the imputation* whether we be transported in mind, *it is* to God: or whether we be sober, *it is* for you. For the charity of Christ presseth us: judging this, that if one died for all, then all were dead. And Christ died for all: that they also, who live, may not now live to themselves, but unto him who died for them and rose again. Wherefore henceforth we know no man according to the flesh. And if we

*of fanaticism, it is so as not to give you scandal.* Either of these explanations of the verse will suit the context; but the first perhaps is better as explaining the words of the preceding verse, " *We commend not ourselves* . . ."

**14.** *presseth,* that is, *constraineth us,* or, *acts as a check on us.*

*if one died for all, then all were dead* (εἰς ὑπὲρ πάντων ἀπέθανεν, ἄρα οἱ πάντες ἀπέθανον). The true translation of the Greek is, "*one died for all, therefore all died.*" The meaning is either:—

(1) Christ died for all, therefore all ought to die to their old life, and live the life of justice.

(2) Christ died for all, because all had died in Adam (cf. 1 Cor. xv. 22).

(3) Christ died for all. and so all died as represented in Him.

Of these interpretations the first would only amount to what is stated in the next verse, which, however, seems to be intended as an additional statement. Moreover, it gives an unnatural rendering to the words *all died*, which, it seems, ought to be as extensive as the expression *for all* of the first clause, where the meaning is universal. Either of the other two explanations is possible, but the latter is decidedly preferable, because the word ἄρα *(then)*, is better suited by the rendering "*therefore*" than by "*because*," and also on account of the context of the passage. If this meaning be accepted, it will denote that our Lord died as the head and representative of humanity, and so humanity, i.e., the human race as a whole, died in Him.

**15.** *who died for them, and rose again.* Christ our Lord has done two things for us; first, He has died for us, and secondly, He has risen again for us. As then all men have been made partners in His death, so His will is that they should become partakers of His life. And this they do when they mortify all their inclinations to sin, and deny themselves for His sake, living only to do His will, and to promote his glory (cf. Rom. vi. 11; Gal. ii. 19, 20). The clause would be better translated "*who died and rose again for them*" (τῷ ὑπὲρ αὐτῶν ἀποθανόντι καὶ ἐγερθέντι).

**16.** *according to the flesh.* These words have been taken in two ways: either as qualifying the verb *know*, that is to say, *we know no man, not even Christ, in a natural or carnal manner;* or as qualifying the thing known: *we know no man, not even Christ, as He is, or was in the flesh.* If we take them in the first way the verse means: *Being dead to ourselves and living only to Christ, we are determined from henceforth to regard and esteem no man according to the purely natural* have known Christ according to the flesh: but now we know him so no longer. If then any be in Christ a new *creature, the old things are passed away, behold all things are made new.*

But all things *are* of God, who hath reconciled us to himself by Christ, and hath given to us the ministry of

<small>*affections of our hearts, but to be guided in our intercourse with every man by supernatural motives alone.* And even if we have known Christ according to mere human affection, as the other apostles did when He was present among them (cf. Matt. xvi. 23), *now this by the power of the Holy Ghost has ceased.* The difficulty of this interpretation is that as St. Paul did not know our Lord during His mortal life, it becomes necessary to suppose that by *we* he means the apostles in general — and this seems to be contrary to the whole tenor of the context, in which he is concerned entirely with a personal defence of himself. It seems better, therefore, to suppose that St. Paul means: *From henceforth we know and esteem no man according to what he is in the flesh, that is, with regard to his nationality, or wealth, or intellect, but only considering what he is in the sight of God. And even if we have taken any pleasure in the thought that our Lord is our own countryman, we are determined now to reject that imperfection, and to view Him only as the Incarnate God and the Redeemer of the world* (cf. Rom. ix. 5; Col. iii. 11).

17. *if then any be in Christ a new creature.* . . . This verse concludes what has been said in the preceding. Those who are renewed by the Passion and Resurrection of our Lord, cease to be swayed by those earthly considerations which previously influenced them, but all their thoughts and actions are regulated by new and supernatural motives. The meaning of this clause is: *if any man be living in union with Christ, there is in his case a new creation.*

*a new creature.* When Adam sinned he lost original justice, and a new creation became necessary, not in the order of nature, but in that of grace. For creation is the bringing into being out of nothing, and he who lacks grace is (in the supernatural order) nothing. So the wicked man is called "him that is not" (Job xviii. 15); and St. Paul said, "If I have not charity, I am nothing" (1 Cor. xiii. 2). Consequently the infusion of grace is a sort of creation; and if any man is thus created anew, the "old things" have passed away for him. These "old things" include the ceremonial observances of the law of Moses (cf. Rom. vii. 6), as well as the corruptions of sin (Rom. vi. 4-6).

18-21. St. Paul, having spoken in the preceding verses (9-17) of the zeal for souls and detachment from the world which is aroused in him by the fear of God and by the hope of the resurrection, now shows that God is the author of all this. Therefore St. Paul presents himself to the Corinthians, not in his own name, but only as God's ambassador.

18. *who hath reconciled us to himself.* God has reconciled mankind to Himself, by freeing men from sin which made them His enemies;</small>

19 reconciliation. For God indeed was in Christ reconciling the world to himself, not imputing to them their sins, and he hath placed in us the word of reconciliation.
20 For Christ therefore we are ambassadors, God as it were exhorting by us. For Christ, we beseech you be reconciled
21 to God. Him, that knew no sin, for us he hath made sin, that we might be made the justice of God in him.

and this He has done through the Incarnate Word (cf. Col. i. 12-23; Rom. v. 10). And not only has He done this objectively, but He has also given a special office to the apostles, his vicars on earth, to proclaim this reconciliation to all the world, and to administer it to all men in the Sacraments of Baptism and Penance (cf. Matt. xxviii. 18-20; Mark xvi. 15, 16, 20).

*us . . . to us:* that is, either the apostles in general, or St. Paul himself. The following verse explains that it is as part of the whole world that the apostles are reconciled.

**19.** *God was in Christ.* . . . The word "*God*" here probably means the Father. It may be understood in one of two ways: either, *God the Father was in Christ, reconciling the world.* . . . i.e., by unity of essence, as our Lord says (John xiv. 10, 11), "I am in the Father, and the Father in me"; or else, *God was reconciling the world to himself in* (or, *through*) *Christ.* Probably the latter explanation is the true one.

*not imputing.* That is, remitting the sins of those who are penitent; not keeping them in His memory to punish them.

V. **20-VI. 10.** In this passage (which is unfortunately broken by the commencement of a new chapter) St. Paul concludes that portion of the Epistle which is devoted to the magnifying of his ministry, by urging the Corinthians to take advantage of it. For he has exercised it with much suffering, and with great power of God.

**20.** *for Christ.* Christ has earned this reconciliation, and proclaimed it to the world.

*ambassadors.* St. Paul is *ambassador for Christ*, because he bears His Person, and speaks in His name and by His power (Matt. x. 20; 2 Cor. xiii. 3).

*be reconciled.* Though God has reconciled all mankind on His part, and in intention, yet He has left to man the exercise of free-will, by which he can either accept the reconciliation through Faith and Penance, or reject it.

**21.** *knew*—that is, by experience.

*he hath made him sin.* This may mean, according to the Hebrew idiom, *hath made Him a sin-offering*, or sacrifice for sin. But it probably has a stronger meaning, namely, *He hath made Him the representative of sin*, on whom the burden of the sins of the whole world was heaped, as if He were sin personified, so that in His death sins died in their collectivity. Another interpretation of the words is that they mean *made him appear as a sinner*, but this is not so probable.

## CHAPTER VI.

AND we helping do exhort you, that you receive not the grace of God in vain. For he saith: *In an accepted time have I heard thee: and in the day of salvation have I helped thee.* Behold, now is the acceptable time: behold now is the day of salvation. Giving no offence to any man, that our ministry be not blamed: but in all things let us exhibit ourselves as the ministers of

*justice of God* is the justice which God gives, as opposed to that in which a man trusts in his own merits, and tries to make himself just without the co-operation of God's grace (cf. Rom. x. 3). St. Paul uses the noun "*justice*" instead of such an expression as "*that we might be made just*," both to mark the antithesis with "*sin*" in the former clause, and also to signify that in Christ we become truly inwardly justified: justice permeates our whole being, if we inhere, by Faith and Charity, in Him who is Justice itself.

### CHAPTER VI.

**1.** *and we helping.* . . . There is no break here in the subject-matter. This verse follows immediately on v. 20 (v. 21 being parenthetical). *We beseech you, be reconciled to God.* . . . *We exhort you that you receive not the grace of God in vain.*

*helping*—that is, either "*helping Christ*," whose ambassadors we are (v. 20), by forwarding the work of reconciliation which He has on His side accomplished; or "*helping God*," acting as His coadjutors in the work of reconciliation (cf. 1 Cor. iii. 9).

*in vain*, i.e., by not corresponding with grace.

**2.** *for he saith.* . . . This verse is parenthetical. It is quoted from Isa. xlix. 8, where God addresses these words to the Messiah pleading and suffering for sinful humanity. The moment is now come of which we were assured by the prophet. The Messiah has appeared. God has heard His prayers, and has supported Him in the day of His suffering, which is the day of our salvation.

*he saith*, that is, God, speaking in the Scriptures.

*accepted . . . acceptable*; rather, "*accepted*" . . . "*most accepted.*" It means the time which is accepted and approved of by God.

**3.** *giving no offence* (cf. 1 Cor. ix. 12; x. 32, 33), that is avoiding everything that might offend any one. These words resume what was said in verse 1, and the participle *to* therefore dependent on the verb "*exhort.*"

**4.** *let us exhibit.* (cf. iv. 2). The Greek (συνιστάνοντες ἑαυτούς) means "*exhibiting*," or "*commending ourselves*," so that it is parallel with "*helping*" (v. 1), and "*giving no offence*" (v. 3).

*as the ministers of God.* In the Greek the word "*ministers*" is in the nominative case. The meaning therefore is, *commending ourselves, as ministers of God should do.*

God, in much patience, in tribulation, in necessities, in
5 distresses, in stripes, in prisons, in seditions, in labours,
6 in watchings, in fastings, in chastity, in knowledge, in
long-suffering, in sweetness, in the Holy Ghost, in charity
7 unfeigned, in the word of truth, in the power of God;

**4-10.** These verses bring out various marks of the true ministers of God.

**4.** *in much patience.* Patience is a mark of the minister of Christ. St. Paul points to nine occasions on which it is exercised. The first three are general, the next three are particular cases of trials from without, and the last three are occasions of voluntary suffering.

*tribulations, necessities, distresses.* Each of these words is stronger than the preceding. The word *distresses* is an apparent, though, of course, not a real, contradiction of iv. 8.

**5.** *stripes,* cf. xi. 23-25.

*prisons.* We only have the record of one imprisonment of St. Paul previous to this time, namely, that at Philippi (Acts xvi. 23), but, no doubt, there had been many others. Pope St. Clement, in his epistle to the Corinthians, says that St. Paul was imprisoned seven times.

*seditions,* or tumults—that is, popular riots like that at Ephesus (see Acts xix. : cf. Acts xiii. 50 ; xiv. 5, 18 ; xvii. 5-8, 13 ; &c.).

*labours,* voluntarily undertaken in the exercise of his ministry.

*fastings* (νηστείαις). Some Protestant commentators have supposed that St. Paul here means involuntary fasting through want of food; but, in the first place, this is not the natural meaning of the Greek word, and secondly, it seems to be excluded by xi. 27, where he speaks of hunger and thirst undergone through necessity, as well as of voluntary fasting.

**6.** *in chastity* (ἐν ἁγνότητι). Some commentators would translate the Greek by "*purity of mind,*" or by "*detachment*" from creatures : but it is more in accordance with the meaning of the Greek to take it as meaning *chastity* in the stricter sense.

*in knowledge,* that is, the knowledge he had acquired for the glory of God in the exercise of his ministry.

*in sweetness,* that is, *benignity* or *considerateness* for others (cf. I Cor. ix. 22).

*in the Holy Ghost,* that is, in the various gifts of the Holy Ghost, but particularly in those special gifts called Charismata, which were common in the apostolic times, and would be another confirmation of the apostolic authority (cf. I Cor. xii. and xiv.).

*in charity unfeigned,* cf. 1 John iii. 18.

**7.** *in the word of truth,* i.e., the preaching of the Gospel, which is the very Truth (cf. ii. 17 ; iv. 2 ; Col. i. 5).

*in the power of God,* i.e., in all that shows our work to be divine, whether the working of miracles (which are commonly called "*powers*" in the New Testament), or the superhuman zeal and courage of the apostles in their labours.

by the armour of justice on the right hand and on the left, by honour and dishonour, by evil report and good 8 report: as deceivers, and yet true: as unknown, and yet known: as dying, and behold we live: as chastised, and 9 not killed: as sorrowful, yet always rejoicing: as needy, 10 yet enriching many: as having nothing, and possessing all things.

Our mouth is open to you, O ye Corinthians, our heart 11

*by the armour of justice*, that is, the weapons used in the cause of justice (cf. x. 4; Eph. vi. 11–17; 1 Thess. v. 8).

*on the right hand and on the left*, that is either, (1) armour protecting the whole body on all sides; or (2) offensive arms in the right hand, such as sword or spear; and the shield for defence on the left.

**8.** *by honour and dishonour.* He commends his ministry by the way in which he endures being reviled, and slandered, &c., as well as by his conduct in the opposite case.

*as deceivers, and yet true*, i.e., *regarded as impostors, but in reality true* (cf. Matt. xxvii. 63).

*as unknown* . . ., i.e., *despised as poor and obscure, but really well known to all true Christians.*

**9.** *as dying* . . ., i.e., *often reported to be at the point of death, if not actually dead: but still preserved in life by God.*

*as chastised* . . ., i.e., *seeming to be chastised by God, because of the great afflictions we undergo unjustly from men, and yet in reality protected by Him from being put to death.*

**10.** *as sorrowful* . . ., i.e., *looked upon as wretched because of our sufferings, but really rejoicing in them* (cf. Acts v. 41).

*as needy, yet enriching many* . . . i.e., *appearing to be in want;* (i.) temporally, yet really provided for by the faithful in all his necessities, *and enriching many* by collecting alms (viii., ix ); (ii.) spiritually, *seeming to be deserted by God*, who allowed Him to suffer, *yet really receiving grace for the benefit and consolation of others* (i. 4, 6).

*as having nothing, and possessing all things*, i.e., *having given up all for Christ, but possessing and enjoying all goods both spiritual and temporal*, because he possessed Christ, who included them all.

VI. 11–VII. 16. Having finished the long passage in which he has vindicated the character of his office, St. Paul now makes a direct appeal to the Corinthians to be generous in the service of God and in respect and obedience to His ministers, and at the same time expresses his joy at the progress they have made in penitence.

**11.** *our mouth is open to you.* That is, *we speak openly, candidly, and fearlessly, all that is in our heart.*

*our heart is enlarged.* He refers either (as St. Thomas says) to his

12 is enlarged. You are not straitened in us: but in your
13 own bowels you are straitened. But having the same
recompense (I speak as to my children) be you also
enlarged.
14 Bear not the yoke with unbelievers. For what participation hath justice with injustice? Or what fellowship
15 hath light with darkness. And what concord hath Christ
with Belial? Or what part hath the faithful with the
16 unbeliever? And what agreement hath the temple of

joy in them, or (as St. Chrysostom says) to his love for them (cf. Ps. cxviii. 32).

**12.** *you are not straitened in us* . . ., i.e., *I am not of narrow heart towards you, but I give you my whole love; but you are straitened in your love to me.* In his former Epistle St. Paul had seemed to be imposing narrow restrictions on his converts. He is now going to expose himself to a similar charge by forbidding intercourse and marriage between them and the heathen. He therefore anticipates this by protesting that he is not lacking in love for them, and by calling upon them to make a generous requital of his love.

**13.** *having.* This word is not in the Greek. The meaning is "*according to the same recompense,*" that is, *in requital of my generous love of you, give me your love. You are my children, and it is the duty of children to repay the love of their father by a return of love.*

**VI. 14–VII. 1.** After the appeal made to the Corinthians in *vv.* 11–13, St. Paul recurs to the subject of *v.* 1, which he proceeds to apply to their special circumstances. Their great danger lies in too close intercourse with the heathen. In his former epistle the apostle has already warned them against mixed marriages (vii. 39), and against participation in idol-feasts (x. 14–28).

**14.** *bear not the yoke* (μὴ γίνεσθε ἑτεροζυγοῦντες ἀπίστοις), that is, "*bear not the yoke unequally with unbelievers,*" or, *have no close fellowship with the heathen.* In this and the two following verses, Christianity is contrasted with heathenism in respect of (1) morals, (2) faith, (3) the leaders of each, (4) their followers, (5) their character and operation. It has been pointed out that the selection of five different words to express the meaning of *fellowship*, shows St. Paul's intimate acquaintance with the Greek language.

*light* is often used to mean Truth (cf. John i.).

**15.** *Belial* means *worthlessness* or *nothingness.* It was applied to the devil as a title of contempt by the Jews; and it is here used to express that the devil is the founder and head of heathenism.

**16.** *the temple of God.* In 1 Cor. vi. 19, St. Paul said that the bodies of Christians are the temple of the Holy Ghost, who dwells in them by the operations of grace. But the apostle uses here the singular number ("*You are the temple*") to denote that though each of them is a temple or shrine of God, yet they are so not in separation

God with idols? For you are the temple of the living God: as God saith: *I will dwell in them, and walk among them, and I will be their God, and they shall be my people.* Wherefore, *Go out from among them, and be ye separate,* saith the Lord, *and touch not the unclean thing. And I will receive you: and I will be a Father to you: and you shall be my sons and daughters, saith the Lord Almighty.*

## CHAPTER VII.

HAVING therefore these promises, dearly beloved, let us cleanse ourselves from all defilement of the

from, or independently of, the rest of the Church, but in such a way that the whole Church constitutes one Temple of God (cf. Eph. ii. 20–22; 1 Pet. ii. 5, &c.)

*the living God.* This expression is used to mark the contrast between the true God and the idols, who have no life in themselves, and so can impart none to their worshippers.

*I will dwell in them.* . . . This quotation is taken from both Lev. xxvi. 11, 12, and Ezech. xxxvii. 27: though it does not quite agree verbally with either passage. In the former God promised to dwell in the midst of the Israelites in the tabernacle. This promise was fulfilled in the Shechinah (see note on iii. 7), which, as the visible representation of God's presence under the form of a fiery cloud rested upon the tabernacle, and afterwards upon the Temple (Exod. xl. 31–36; Lev. xvi. 2; 3 Kings viii. 10, 11; cf. Isa. vi. 4; Agg. ii. 4–10). In the latter place, God makes a similar promise prophetically through Ezechiel with respect to the Church, in which He promises to dwell for ever.

**17.** *go out from among them.* . . . This quotation is taken from Isa. lii. 11, where the Jews are warned not to defile themselves with the impurities of the Babylonians.

**18.** *I will be a Father to you.* . . . This passage is generally quoted as from the prophet Jeremias xxxi. 9, where God promises the restoration of the Israelites: but the words resemble more closely the promise made to David (2 Kings vii. 14), with regard to his son Solomon, who was to build the temple.

*and daughters.* It is probable that St. Paul adds these words to his quotation because one of the chief modes of intercourse with the heathen, which he wished the Christians to avoid, was mixed marriages.

## CHAPTER VII.

**1.** This verse concludes the passage commencing in vi. 14.

*these promises,* namely those mentioned above, that God will dwell flesh and of the spirit, perfecting sanctification in the fear of God.

2, 3 Receive us. We have injured no man, we have corrupted no man, we have overreached no man. I speak not this to your condemnation. For we have said before, that you are in our hearts, to die together, and to live 4 together. Great is my confidence with you, great is my glorying for you. I am filled with comfort: I exceedingly abound with joy in all our tribulation.

5 For also when we were come into Macedonia, our flesh

in the midst of His Church, and that the faithful shall be His temple and His children. As these promises have now received their fulfilment, so we must also fulfil our obligations by cleansing ourselves from all the bodily and spiritual defilement of heathenism; for impurity has no part in the Temple of God, and we must in the fear of God constantly strive after ever greater sanctification, perfecting, as St. Thomas says, the sanctification which was begun by our Baptism.

**2–4.** St. Paul recurs to the subject of vi. 11–13, and now calls on the Corinthians to enlarge their hearts to receive him, and expresses his confidence that they will do so; a confidence which is based on the good news he has of them from Titus.

**2.** *receive us* (χωρήσατε ἡμᾶς). The Greek naturally means "*Make room for us in your hearts*"; and it is taken in this sense by Sts. Chrysostom and Ambrose. It refers to vi. 12.

*we have injured no man*; as the false teachers had done by claiming authority to which they had no right, and by teaching false doctrine.

*corrupted*, by leading them into evil through bad example.

*overreached*, by defrauding them in any way of their goods, as his opponents did, and as he may have been accused of doing because of the collections of alms he had made at Corinth (cf. xii. 17, 18).

**3.** *I speak not this to your condemnation*, that is, I am not speaking as though you had accused me of these things, or as though you had given credit to the charges brought against me.

*we have said before*, i.e., vi. 11.

*you are in our hearts* . . . The words have been explained in two different ways. They mean either *you are in my heart, so that I wish to live and to die with you*: or else *you are in my heart, so as to remain united with me in love whether I die or whether I live*. Most commentators take it in the former way.

**4.** *I am filled with comfort* . . . These words refer to what follows, namely the news of the repentance and amendment of the Corinthians, which was the source of the greatest comfort and joy to St. Paul.

**5–16.** St. Paul here continues the narrative, which has been interrupted since ii. 13 chiefly by the long passage (ii. 14–vi. 10), in which had no rest, but we suffered all tribulation; combats without, fears within. But God, who comforteth the humble, ⁶ comforted us by the coming of Titus. And not by his ⁷ coming only, but also by the consolation, wherewith he was comforted in you, relating to us your desire, your mourning, your zeal for me, so that I rejoiced the more.

For although I made you sorrowful by my epistle, ⁸ I do not repent: and if I did repent, seeing that the same epistle (although but for a time) did make you sorrowful: now I am glad: not because you were made ⁹

he wrote in praise of his apostolic office. He had said in chap. ii. that he could not rest at Troas because of his anxiety to get news from Titus about the Corinthian Church, and so he went on into Macedonia to meet him. Now he says that even on reaching Macedonia he still had no peace until Titus arrived, and brought good news of them.

5. *our flesh.* That is, although his higher nature, including his will, rested in God and was perfectly resigned to Him, yet his lower nature was disturbed, and found no comfort.

*combats without,* from the opponents of Christianity.

*fears within,* with respect to the different Churches he had founded, and especially that of the Corinthians.

6, 7. The meaning is, *God comforted us by the coming of Titus, and not only by that, but also by the comfort which he received from you, and which he imparted to us, by relating your desire, your mourning, and your zeal.*

7. *your desire,* i.e., to see me.

*your mourning,* i.e., at having grieved me.

*your zeal for me,* i.e, to defend me and my apostolate against my detractors.

*the more.* This may mean either *I rejoiced more at the news he brought, than at his mere coming,* or possibly, *My joy was greater than my previous sorrow, at causing your sadness, had been.*

8. *and if I did repent.* The words (εἰ καί), translated "*and if,*" are the same as those which are translated "*although*" at the beginning of the verse. The word (μεταμέλομαι) translated "*repent*" might be better rendered "*regret.*" It is from a different root from the word translated "*penance*" in the next verse. St. Paul did not indeed repent of what he had said in his first letter, which had been written under the inspiration of the Holy Ghost, and was necessitated by the state of the Corinthian Church; but he greatly regretted the necessity of paining them, especially while he remained in doubt as to whether this sorrow had borne fruit.

9. *according to God,* that is, with a sorrow for sin proceeding from the love of God, in consequence of which they not only suffered no injury from him, but received a great benefit.

sorrowful; but because you were made sorrowful unto penance. For you were made sorrowful according to God, 10 that you might suffer damage by us in nothing. For the sorrow that is according to God worketh penance steadfast unto salvation: but the sorrow of the world worketh death. 11 For behold this self-same thing, that you were made sorrowful according to God, how great carefulness it worketh in you: yea defence, yea indignation, yea fear, yea desire, yea zeal, yea revenge; in all things you have 12 shewed yourselves to be undefiled in the matter. Wherefore although I wrote to you, *it was* not for his sake that

10. *steadfast*, that is a penance which they would not afterwards regret, though it might be painful, because it is the medicine of the soul, which was able to procure their salvation.

*the sorrow of the world* is the sorrow which those, whose affections are fixed on earthly things, feel when they lose the objects of their desire.

11. *carefulness*. St. Thomas observes that when a man is in prosperity he is apt to be negligent, but true sorrow and penance cause great care to avoid sin for the future.

The following words may be taken in pairs thus:—

(1) with regard to themselves:

*defence*, that is, defending themselves against the charge of remissness and carelessness in conniving at the fault of the incestuous man, by exhibiting greater eagerness for good.

*indignation* against themselves, now that they recognized their sin and folly.

(2) with regard to St. Paul:

*fear* of the just wrath of the apostle.

*desire* to manifest their amendment both before God and His apostle.

(3) with regard to the sinner:

*zeal* for God's honour, which led them to excommunicate the sinner at St. Paul's bidding.

*revenge*, i.e. the punishment of the sin.

Some commentators take the *indignation* to be against the sinner. Others take the *fear* to be distrust of themselves, lest relying on their own powers, they might again offend God by sin: and the *revenge* to be revenge of their own sins upon themselves with tears and penances.

We must notice, also, that in this verse the repeated use of "*yea*" denotes the progress of true penance. It is equivalent to "*and moreover*."

Carefulness is the general spirit which characterizes the whole penitence; and the other characteristics, when found together, prove its completeness.

12. *it was not* . . . i.e., this was not the chief cause of our writing

did the wrong, nor for him that suffered it: but to manifest
our carefulness that we have for you, before God: there- 13
fore we were comforted.  But in our consolation we did
the more abundantly rejoice for the joy of Titus, because 14
his spirit was refreshed by you all.  And if I have boasted
anything to him of you, I have not been put to shame,
but as we have spoken all things to you in truth, so also
our boasting that was made to Titus, is found truth.  And 15
his bowels are more abundantly towards you; remembering
the obedience of you all, how with fear and trembling you
received him.  I rejoice that in all things I have confidence 16
in you.

*for him that suffered it*, that is, the father whose wife had been taken by his son (1 Cor. v. 1).

*but to manifest our carefulness* . . . St. Paul's main reason for writing was his care for the Church at Corinth in general, both to elicit evidence of the fact that they had not as a body connived at the act of fornication, and to move to penance those who had been partially guilty in this respect.

*our carefulness that we have for you.*  Many of the Greek MSS. have "*your carefulness for us.*"  If this reading be accepted the meaning will be that St. Paul wrote to give an opportunity for them to show in God's sight the care they had for him.

**13.** *therefore we were comforted*, namely, when he heard of their penance and their zeal.

*in our consolation* . . . that is, the consolation he felt at their repentance was increased by the joy which it caused to Titus.

**14.** *our boasting that was made to Titus.* . . . St. Paul expresses his joy that what he had said in their praise to Titus, before his mission to them, has not been proved false by their conduct, but just as whatever he had said to them was true, so what he had said to Titus about them, Titus has found to be true.  Many commentators suppose that the things which St. Paul here says that he had spoken to them in truth, were his praises of Titus, which they had found true when Titus visited them.

**15.** *his bowels are more abundantly towards you*, i.e., *his love for you is the greater when he recalls the promptitude with which you obeyed him, when he brought you my commands.*

**16.** *I rejoice that in all things I have confidence in you.*  St. Paul means that he is glad that their conduct has shown that he can trust them to receive necessary admonitions in the proper spirit, so that he will have no fear in future in reproving them or warning them when necessary, or in saying anything that he may judge to be to their profit, since he now knows by experience that they will receive it in a spirit of obedience as his true children.

# PART II., CHAPS. VIII., IX.

IN these two chapters St. Paul exhorts the Corinthians to collect alms for the poor at Jerusalem, and takes the occasion to give them a short instruction on almsgiving.

The apparent abruptness of the introduction of this subject is explained by the fact that he has already mentioned it in his former letter (1 Cor. xvi. 1-3), so that no prefatory remarks are now required. The reason why the subject is brought in at this point of the Epistle is partly, perhaps, that the mention in the last chapter of his coming into Macedonia naturally leads him to speak of the liberality of the Macedonians. But a stronger reason is found in the consideration of the sequence of events. It was necessary that he should ascertain the goodness of their dispositions and the sincerity of their penance, and write words calculated to complete in them, if necessary, the work of grace, before he could mention this subject with any profit; for if he had urged them to almsgiving earlier, they would either have refused to listen to him, or at least they would have lost a large part of the merit of the good work for want of the proper dispositions. As soon, therefore, as he has secured these dispositions, he proceeds to introduce the subject of these two chapters.

The object of the collection was to relieve the poor Christians at Jerusalem. Their poverty was due to various causes. There was a great disturbance at this time throughout Judea owing to popular tumults, which caused distress. Moreover Christian converts were often persecuted and disowned by their Jewish relatives (cf. Heb. x. 34). For these reasons alms were frequently given by other churches for their relief (cf. Acts xi. 29, 30; xxiv. 17; Gal. ii. 10; Rom. xv. 25-27).

## *SUMMARY.*

(i) St. Paul sets before the Corinthians the example of the liberality of the Macedonians . . . . . viii. 1-5
(ii) And exhorts them to follow it . . . . . 6-8
(iii) He puts before them the example of our Lord, as a motive to make them prompt in giving . . . 9-12
(iv) He shows that he does not ask their alms out of any undue favour to the Christians at Jerusalem . . 10 15
(v) He writes to commend Titus and his companions to them . . . . . . . . . 16-24
(vi) He urges them to give promptly and generously . . ix. 1-9
(vii) Finally he shows the great advantage and merit of almsgiving . . . . . . . . 10-15

# CHAPTER VIII.

NOW we make known unto you, brethren, the grace of God, that hath been given in the churches of Macedonia; that in much experience of tribulation they have had abundance of joy, and their very deep poverty hath abounded unto the riches of their simplicity. For according to their power, (I bear them witness,) and beyond their power, they were willing; with much entreaty begging of us the grace and communication of the ministry that is done toward the saints. And not as we

**1-8.** St. Paul exhorts the Corinthians to follow the example of the liberality of the Macedonians.

**1.** *grace of God*, that is, the grace which had inspired the Macedonians with joy in suffering, and which had led them to liberality in giving alms.

**2.** *in much experience* . . . i.e., the genuine and supernatural character of their joy was demonstrated by the fact of its being abundantly maintained in affliction.

*their very deep poverty hath abounded* . . . This is explained by v. 12. The abundance of their alms was shown in their willingness more than in actual quantity. In like manner our Lord said of the widow who cast into the treasury her whole living, which was one farthing, that she had cast in more than all the rich people who gave largely of their wealth (Mark xii. 43).

*simplicity.* This word denotes the purity of their intention in giving, namely, that they gave readily and cheerfully without grudging (cf. ix. 11, 13; Rom. xii. 8).

**4.** *begging of us the grace* . . . i.e., entreating to be allowed a share in this work, and to have a part in relieving the want of the Christians at Jerusalem. For they regarded it as a great grace to be allowed the opportunity of gaining merit by so doing.

*saints.* Cf. note on i. 1.

**5.** *not as we hoped*, that is, they surpassed his hopes: not merely in the amount they gave, and their willingness in giving, but also in

hoped, but they gave their own selves first to the Lord,
6 then to us by the will of God: insomuch, that we desired Titus, that as he had begun, so also he would finish
7 among you this same grace: that as in all things you abound in faith, and word, and knowledge, and all carefulness: moreover also in your charity towards us, so in
8 this grace also you may abound. I speak not as commanding: but by the carefulness of others, approving also the good disposition of your charity.
9 For you know the grace of our Lord JESUS CHRIST,

the purity of their intention. For their intention was not, as he had expected, merely to make satisfaction for their sins, but pure devotion to God, to whom they had given first themselves, and then their alms as an acknowledgment of His complete sovereignty over their hearts. It cannot be supposed that St. Paul had anticipated that they would give from a bad or worthless motive, for, in that case, he would not have asked for their alms; and consequently we may conclude from this passage that motives which are good, though not the best, have merit in God's sight.

**6.** *insomuch that* . . . i.e., we were so affected by this example of liberality that we asked Titus to collect alms in Corinth, a work which he had begun on his first visit.

**7.** *word and knowledge.* Cf. 1 Cor. i. 5.

*word* may mean the confession of your faith, but it is more probable that it means the Christian Truth considered objectively, while *knowledge* is the subjective apprehension of the same.

**8.** *I speak not as commanding.* Though St. Paul has called this almsgiving a great grace, still he is unwilling to use his apostolic power to order the Corinthians to give beyond what is of strict obligation. But, though he does not command this, yet he puts before them the example of the Macedonians, who were so careful to help the poor, that he may prove whether they have an equally good disposition (cf. note on v. 13).

**9.** *for you know.* . . . In this verse he quotes the example of our Lord, in addition to that of the Macedonians.

*the grace of our Lord*, that is, the benefit which He has freely given us.

*being rich.* St. Paul says "*being rich*" instead of "*having been rich*," because our Lord did not lay aside the riches of His Divinity when He took upon Himself the poverty of our human nature, although His Divine glory and attributes remained concealed under the form of a servant (cf. Phil. ii. 5–8).

*through his poverty.* Our Lord enriched us by the destitution of all temporal things, to which He submitted in His Incarnation, and throughout His earthly life, in two ways:

that being rich he became poor for your sakes; that
through his poverty you might be rich. And herein I 10
give my advice: for this is profitable for you, who have
begun not only to do, but also to be willing, a year ago:
now therefore perform ye it also in deed; that, as your 11
mind is forward to be willing, so it may be also to
perform, out of that which you have. For if the will be 12
forward, it is accepted according to that which *a man*
hath, not according to that which he hath not. For *I* 13
*mean* not that others should be eased, and you burthened:
but by an equality. In this present time let your abun- 14

(1) by way of example, that we may be led to imitate Him in
the love of poverty, and that we may be moved to be charitable
towards the poor, who most resemble Him and are most loved by Him
(cf. Jas. ii. 5; Matt. xxv. 40; Luke vi. 20).

(2) by sacramental efficacy. As by dying a natural death He gave
to men eternal life, so by suffering want in temporal things, He has
given men all spiritual wealth.

**10.** *I give my advice.* This is contrasted with the command mentioned in *v.* 8.

*this is profitable for you.* This is a third reason to urge them to
liberality. He has already put before them the example of the Macedonians, and that of our Lord; now he points out that it will be
profitable to themselves, because of the merit they will gain thereby.

*who have begun*, i.e., *who were the first* (that is, before the Macedonians) *not only in acting, but also in being ready to act.*

*a year ago*, that is, "*since last year*" (cf. ix. 2). It need not mean
that so much as a year had elapsed.

**11.** *out of that which you have*, that is, "*in proportion to what you have.*"

**12.** *it is accepted,* that is, the will is accepted.

**13.** *I mean.* These words are supplied by the English translators
to complete the sense. But it would be better to supply some such
words as "*this collection is not made.*" St. Paul means, *I do not
require of you to give such alms as would leave you burthened and
afflicted.* The Macedonians indeed had been ready to give even
beyond their power, but this is not to be asked of any one who does
not offer it of his own accord. Therefore all that St. Paul asks is that
they should give of their abundance, to supply the needs of their
brethren, for this much Christian charity requires.

**14.** *your abundance.* Corinth was an important centre of trade,
and a wealthy town, and though it is true that the Christian converts
were not generally from the most wealthy classes (1 Cor. i. 26), still
they must have included many who were well able to give large alms.

*that their abundance also may supply your want.* Some modern

dance supply their want: that their abundance also may
15 supply your want, that there may be an equality. As
it is written: *He that had much, had nothing over: and
he that had little, had no want.*

16 And thanks be to God, who hath given the same care-
17 fulness for you in the heart of Titus. For indeed he accep-

commentators have supposed that these words mean no more than that, when you are in want of alms, the Christians of Jerusalem will help you in turn. But considering how poor the Church of Jerusalem was, and that there was no prospect of their ever being in a position to give such help to the comparatively wealthy Corinthians, such a meaning is clearly out of the question. Besides, it is equally certain that St. Paul would not ask the Corinthians to give alms only that they might receive as much again, for such a motive would destroy all the merit of their action (cf. Luke vi..33; xiv. 12–14). It is therefore certain that we must take this passage, as it is taken by all the Fathers, to mean that their abundance of graces may supply your spiritual wants, and their prayers may bring you after your death to paradise (cf. Luke xvi. 9).

**15.** *as it is written.* St. Paul illustrates what he has been saying by a reference to the miraculous gift of the manna to the Israelites in the desert (Exod. xvi. 18). This manna was so ordained by God that, when the Israelites took it to their tents and measured it, whatever any man had gathered, every one was found to have the same measure, namely, one gomor. As God thus made the measure equal for all, so it is right for Christians to preserve the same equality, by those who are rich, sharing their wealth, whether temporal or spiritual, with those in want.

**16-24.** These verses contain a commendation of the three messengers whom St. Paul was sending to collect the alms of the Corinthians. This commendation was necessary in order to assure the Corinthians that they came with authority from him. It was also necessary, as he explains (*vv.* 19, 20), that he should send messengers accredited by the Churches, as well as one appointed by himself, to prevent any accusation being made against his own honesty in the collection—to such an extent had his enemies carried their malice against him!

**16.** *the same*, that is, the same as St. Paul himself had for them.

**17.** *he accepted the exhortation*, that is to say, though Titus was quite willing and eager to go of his own accord, yet he attended to our exhortation. This is said, either to show his obedience, or to prove to the Corinthians that he was really St. Paul's representative.

*he went* (ἐξῆλθεν). This is an instance of the epistolary aorist (see note on ii. 9). It does not mean that Titus had gone at the time St. Paul was writing, but it regards the time from the point of view of the readers of the letter, so that it means he will have gone to them when they receive and read the letter. The same remark applies to "*we have sent*" in *vv.* 18, 22.

ted the exhortation: but being more careful, of his own will he went unto you. We have sent also with him the brother, whose praise is in the gospel through all the churches: and not that only, but he was also ordained by

**18.** *the brother*, that is, not an actual brother, but a fellow-Christian, as in *v*. 22.

*whose praise is in the gospel* . . . The "*gospel*" always means in the New Testament the gospel as it was preached, not any one of the written narratives which we possess. Therefore this passage means that the brother was praised for his zeal in preaching and teaching the Christian faith. Numerous conjectures have been made as to who this brother was. The only two names, however, which are supported by the ancients are those of Barnabas and Luke. The former has been supposed by many of the Greek Fathers to be the person meant, because so much of what is here said is suitable to him. There was no one, perhaps, except St. Paul himself, of whom it could so well be said that his praise was in all the Churches. Moreover we know that he had been St. Paul's companion in collecting and bearing alms on a former occasion (Acts xi. 30), and that at the Council of Jerusalem the care of the poor had been specially commended to him (Gal. ii. 9, 10). But on the other hand, St. Barnabas was himself an apostle, and so it is unlikely that he would be sent by St. Paul, and much more unlikely that he would be made second to Titus. Moreover, Paul and Barnabas had separated some years previously (cf. Acts xv. 39), and there is no indication that they had come together again. The other conjecture, namely that this brother was St. Luke, cannot indeed be considered certain, but it is supported by a greater weight both of tradition and of internal evidence. It is maintained by most of the Latin Fathers, as well as by the subscription which was added to the epistle at an early date. It is true that one argument in favour of this supposition is that this verse contains an allusion to his written Gospel, which, as we have seen, is not the case, even if his Gospel had been written at this time. But an argument in favour of this identification is derived from the fact that we gather from Acts xx. 2, 5, that St. Luke was not with St. Paul in his journey from Macedonia to Greece, though he accompanied the apostle on his return; since the latter passage uses the plural "*us*" and the former the singular "*he*." It seems, therefore, on the whole, that St. Luke is more likely than any other person to be the brother here alluded to, though the question cannot be decided with any certainty.

**19.** *ordained* (χειροτονηθείς) *by the churches.* If this means that the "*brother*" had received the sacrament of ordination to be a companion of St. Paul's travels, and to assist him in the ministry of this grace of collecting alms, then we must understand the words "*by the churches*" to mean by the prelates, and with the assent of the laity. In this case the opinion that the brother was St. Barnabas receives additional support, since we know (Acts xiii. 2) that the latter was ordained with St.

the churches companion of our travels, for this grace, which is administered by us to the glory of the Lord, and our
20 determined will: avoiding this lest any man should blame
21 us in this abundance which is administered by us. For we forecast what may be good not only before God, but also
22 before men. And we have sent with them our brother also, whom we have often proved diligent in many things: but now much more diligent, with much confidence in you.
23 Either for Titus, who is my companion and fellow-labourer towards you, or our brethren, the apostles of the churches,

Paul to be a sharer in his missionary labours. The Greek word, however, can also mean "*chosen*," and very many commentators suppose the meaning to be that he was chosen by the Churches (either of Ephesus and Asia, or of Macedonia) to accompany St. Paul in collecting the alms and conveying them to Jerusalem, for the purpose (as is explained in *v.* 20) of preventing any possibility of scandal.

*for this grace*, that is, to procure this grace by collecting the alms.

*our determined will*, that is, to serve our determination by inciting you to give.

**20.** *lest any man should blame us* . . . These words explain why he commends these men, and speaks of their having been chosen by the Churches. It is equivalent to saying, *We have sent men who are well known for their zeal, and who have not been chosen by ourselves, but by the churches* (or, *who have been ordained for this very purpose*); *to exclude all possibility of a suspicion of our integrity in administering this money.*

**21.** *we forecast* . . . that is to say, *We are always ready to provide beforehand what shall be pleasing to God, and at the same time not a scandal to men.*

**22.** *our brother.* Who this third brother was is quite unknown. Some have supposed Apollo, others Silas, others one of the disciples mentioned in Acts xx. 4: but tradition is silent on the point, and the description is not sufficient to enable us to make even a probable conjecture.

*with much confidence in you.* This may mean the confidence which St. Paul had, but it is more likely to be the confidence of this brother.

**23.** *either for Titus.* This verse is somewhat obscure, because of the condensed form of expression used in the Greek. The meaning is, "*whether it be that I write on behalf of Titus, he is my companion*, &c.; *or whether it be our brethren* (namely, the two companions of Titus) *of whom I write, they are the apostles of the churches, and the glory of Christ.*"

*apostles.* This word is not here used in its strict sense, but in a wider meaning. The original meaning of the word is *messengers*, and it probably means here *the messengers sent by the churches*. If so, it follows that the third brother, as well as the second, was chosen by the Churches to accompany Titus (cf. also Phil. ii. 25).

the glory of Christ. Wherefore shew ye to them, in the 24 sight of the churches, the evidence of your charity, and of our boasting on your behalf.

## CHAPTER IX.

FOR concerning the ministry, that is done towards the saints, it is superfluous for me to write unto you. For 2 I know your forward mind: for which I boast of you to the Macedonians, that Achaia also is ready from the year past; and your emulation hath provoked very many. Now 3 I have sent the brethren, that the thing which we boast of concerning you be not made void in this behalf, that (as I have said) you may be ready: lest when the Macedonians 4 shall come with me, and find you unprepared, we (not to say ye) should be ashamed in this matter. Therefore I 5 thought it necessary to desire the brethren that they would

**24.** *in the sight of the churches*, that is to say, by letting them see your liberality, you will be manifesting it to the Churches through their representatives.
*and of our boasting on your behalf*, that is, *justify my praise of you by your liberality*. (Cf. ix. 2.)

### CHAPTER IX.

IX. In this chapter St. Paul turns from the praise of his legates to the subject of the almsgiving. And of this in general he considers it unnecessary for him to say anything (*vv.* 1, 2) in order to urge them to give, but he exhorts them to give promptly (*vv.* 3-5) and generously (6-9), and shows the great profit that will result from their doing so (*vv.* 10-15).
**2.** *Achaia.* Corinth was the metropolis of Achaia, and probably at this time contained the most important Church in that province. See note on i. 1, and Introduction iii. 1.
*your emulation* . . . that is, many have been roused by the example of the Corinthians to emulate them.
**3.** *made void*, that is, that the subject of his boasting may not be nullified, which it would be if the Corinthians failed to carry their will into effect.
**4.** *the Macedonians.* It is probable that some of them would accompany the apostle to assist him on his journey (cf. 1 Cor. xvi. 6).
*we should be ashamed*, that is, if our boasting were proved false.
**5.** *as a blessing, not as covetousness*, that is given freely and spon-

go to you before, and prepare this blessing before promised, to be ready, so as a blessing, not as covetousness.

6. Now this I say: He who soweth sparingly, shall also reap sparingly: and he who soweth in blessings, shall also reap of blessings. 7. Every one as he hath determined in his heart, not with sadness or of necessity: *For God loveth a* 8. *cheerful giver.* And God is able to make all grace abound in you: that ye always having all sufficiency in all things 9. may abound to every good work. As it is written: *He hath dispersed abroad, he hath given to the poor; his justice* 10. *remaineth for ever.* And he that ministereth seed to the

taneously, and not tardily or with any appearance of unwillingness, as though it were being extorted from their covetousness.

**6-11.** In these verses St. Paul urges the Corinthians to give liberally and cheerfully, putting before them the example of the sower, who, though he seems to cast his seed away, in reality reaps a harvest proportioned to, but far exceeding, the amount of his seed.

**6.** *he who soweth sparingly* . . . that is, he who gives little will have little reward, but he who freely scatters many benefits on others will receive many benefits both temporal and spiritual from God.

**7.** *as he hath determined*, that is, according as he is willing, for God does not require so much the gift, as a willing spirit.

*with sadness*, like a covetous man, who grudges to part with his money.

*of necessity*, like a hypocrite, who gives for the sake of appearance, lest he should seem less liberal than others; constrained by his regard for public opinion.

*God loveth a cheerful giver.* These words are quoted freely from the Septuagint version of Prov. xxii. 8.

**8.** *God is able to make all grace abound in you.* St. Paul meets the possible objection that if they gave freely they would themselves be in need, by reminding them of the almighty power of God, which was able to give them all good things. In temporal things He would always give them sufficiency, and together with that the graces necessary for them to abound in all good works.

*God is able* (δυνατεῖ ὁ θεὸς)—that is, *God is powerful.*

**9.** *he hath dispersed abroad.* This quotation is from Ps. cxi. 9. The subject of this verse is evidently not God, as in *v.* 8, but the charitable man.

*dispersed abroad*, that is, *scattered*, as a sower scatters his seed.

*his justice*, that is, *his alms* (cf. Matt. vi. 1). His alms are called justice because they are acts of justice. So the meaning is that, though scattered, they are not lost, but remain and bear fruit like seed cast into the ground (cf. Eccles. xi. 1).

**10.** *he that ministereth seed* . . . It is God who gave them the opportunity to do good. If they corresponded with this grace, He would no sower, will both give you bread to eat, and will multiply your seed, and increase the growth of the fruits of your justice: that being enriched in all things, you may abound ¹¹ unto all simplicity, which worketh through us thanksgiving to God.  Because the administration of this office doth ¹² not only supply the want of the saints, but aboundeth also by many thanksgivings in the Lord.  By the proof of ¹³ this ministry, glorifying God for the obedience of your confession unto the gospel of Christ, and for the simplicity of your communicating unto them, and unto all, and in their praying for you, being desirous of you because ¹⁴ of the excellent grace of God in you.  Thanks be to God for his unspeakable gift.

only provide them with sufficiency for themselves, but also increased opportunities of almsgiving, as well as growth in justice. The sower is supposed to be a labourer whose master supplies him with the seed to sow, and gives him both sustenance during his work, and also a share in the harvest. The harvest itself is partly fresh seed for the coming year, partly the fruits of the first seed intended for food. So God gives three things to those who are generous in almsgiving:

(1) *bread*, that is, a sufficiency of all temporal and spiritual gifts for their immediate needs.

(2) *seed*, that is, enlarged opportunities of almsgiving, and so of gaining fresh merit, and winning a greater reward.

(3) *fruits of justice*, in greater justice, by growth in virtue and holiness.

**11.** *simplicity*, that is, *sincere liberality*, as in viii. 2, &c.

*which worketh* . . . Either, *your liberality causes us to thank God*, or more probably, *your alms, dispensed by us, cause the poor at Jerusalem to give thanks to God*.

**12.** *the administration of this office*. It is not quite certain whether the *administrators* here referred to are the Corinthians, who gave the alms, or St. Paul and his companions, who carried them to Jerusalem.

*of this office* (τῆς λειτουργίας ταύτης). The Greek word means a public service rendered to the state, and so can be applied to a benefit bestowed on the Church.

**13.** *by the proof of this ministry*. Either, *having had proof of your ministration of alms to them*, or, *having had proof of your liberality through our administration of these alms*.

*the obedience of your confession*, that is, their obedience to the Christian faith and the Gospel of Christ, which enjoins charity towards the poor.

**14.** *desirous of you*. Either, *desirous of your spiritual good*, or *desirous of seeing you*.

**15.** *thanks be to God for his unspeakable gift*. In *vv.* 8–10 St. Paul proved what profit would result to the Corinthians from generosity in almsgiving; in *vv*. 11–14 he shows how God will be glorified thereby, and the Christians at Jerusalem will be benefited, not only temporally, but also spiritually, because they will be moved to give thanks to God for the graces bestowed on the Corinthians. He now concludes his exhortation by giving thanks to God for the unspeakable gift of His grace, which moved the Corinthians to this liberality, and so caused such countless blessings, redounding both to the glory of God and to the good of the givers and receivers. St. Paul seems to wish in this verse to lead his converts to thank God, from whom alone comes both the opportunity and the grace necessary for a work so profitable and meritorious, lest they might be inclined to pride themselves on their own liberality, and so lose all the merit of their good work.

# PART III., CHAPS. X.-XIII.

## *SUMMARY.*

*He refutes the objections of his adversaries*, x. 1–xiii. 10.

(i.) St. Paul commences this polemical section with a humble but firm appeal to those who have been misled by the false teachers, to return to their obedience to their true apostle, at the same time warning them that he will punish those who remain refractory . . . . . . . x. 1–7

(ii.) He then proceeds to show that he will not be (as his opponents say) less severe when present than when absent . . . . . . . 8–11

(iii.) And he refuses to put himself into comparison with these false apostles who are always commending themselves . . . . . . . 12–18

*Chapters xi.–xiii. contain St. Paul's defence of himself at greater length. He has just said that a man should not praise himself, and therefore he begins—*

(iv.) By explaining his apparent inconsistency which he calls his folly, but which is necessitated by his zeal for them, and the danger in which he sees them placed . . . . . . . xi. 1–4

(v.) He then proceeds to state his proposition—he is not, as his opponents maintain, in any way inferior to the other apostles . . . . . . 5, 6

(vi.) In order to prove this thesis, he first refutes the insinuation that he had shown his consciousness of want of authority by taking no pay from them . 7–15

(vii.) Secondly, he declares that he has all the outward marks of which they boast, whilst in what he has done and suffered for Christ's sake he far surpasses them . . . . . . . 16–33

(viii.) Besides all this, he says that he has had visions and revelations of God, of which he might speak, but he prefers to glory only in his weakness . . xii. 1–6

| | | |
|---|---|---|
| (ix.) | Of this weakness he is forcibly reminded by the temptations with which he had to contend, of which he glories most willingly, because of the manifestation of the Divine power through them . | 7–10 |
| (x.) | He concludes this proof of his authority . . | 11–13 |
| (xi.) | And proceeds to say that he will continue to act in the same manner . . . . . . | 14–15 |
| (xii.) | And finally refutes a more subtle form of the calumny on his honesty . . . . . | 16–18 |
| (xiii.) | In conclusion, turning rather to the Church as a whole than to his opponents in particular, he shows that this self-defence has been undertaken not for his own glory but out of necessity, for their spiritual profit and the glory of God . . . | 19–21 |
| (xiv.) | But he says that if any of them continue to allow themselves to be misled by these false teachers he will be obliged to treat them with severity: it is to the desire to avoid this necessity that the sharpness of his letter must be attributed . . . | xiii. 1–10 |
| *Conclusion*—Final exhortation, salutation, and benediction . . . . . . . . . | | xiii. 11–13 |

## CHAPTER X.

NOW I Paul myself beseech you, by the mildness and modesty of Christ, who in presence indeed am lowly among you, but being absent am bold toward you. But I beseech you, that I may not be bold when I am present, with that confidence wherewith I am thought to be ²

## CHAPTER X.

**1.** *I Paul.* In these last chapters St. Paul usually speaks in the singular number, because the attack on him was personal—in the previous chapters he had used the plural, because he wished to defend not only his own apostolate but also that of his colleagues, and the priestly office in general.

*I beseech you.* Bernard of Pecquigny says that St. Paul uses the word *beseech* instead of *command*, because he wishes to teach the proud humility by Christ's example and his own, and by humility to lead them to salvation.

*modesty.* The meaning here is "*gentleness*."

*who in presence indeed am lowly among you.* This was what his opponents said about him (cf. *v.* 10). The word "*indeed*" is here equivalent to "*as they say*."

**2.** *but I beseech you . . .* In this verse we see St. Paul acting in direct opposition to that of which his opponents accused him. Instead of being stern when absent, and timid when present, he is here using entreaty in his letter, that he may not be obliged to exercise authority when he comes to them.

*I am thought* (λογίζομαι). If we adopt this rendering, the meaning is "*that I may not have to exercise that boldness when present which I am supposed to show by my letters when I am absent.*" But in this case we should expect to find some such words as "*when absent*" inserted. The Greek verb may, however, equally well be taken as the middle voice, and in that case the meaning is, "*that I may not be obliged when I come to exercise that authority which I am thinking of exercising against some.*" If we follow this translation it will appear that St. Paul meant to insinuate that he was not yet quite resolved on using stern measures, but was only deliberating about them, and wished to leave his enemies still an opportunity of penance.

bold, against some, who reckon us as if we walked according
3 to the flesh. For though we walk in the flesh, we do not
4 war according to the flesh. For the weapons of our warfare are not carnal, but mighty to God unto the pulling
5 down of fortifications; destroying counsels, and every height that exalteth itself against the knowledge of God; and bringing into captivity every understanding unto the
6 obedience of Christ, and having in readiness to revenge all disobedience, when your obedience shall be fulfilled.
7 See the things that are according to outward appearance. If any man trust to himself, that he is Christ's, let him think this again with himself, that as he is Christ's, so are we also.

*as if we walked according to the flesh:* that is, *as if our conduct was dictated purely by motives of worldly prudence.* They probably called his boldness, arrogance; and attributed his gentleness to a desire to retain power by compromise with the world. These are the identical charges that are still most persistently brought against the Catholic Church and the Apostolic See by their bitterest enemies.

**4.** *the weapons of our warfare,* that is, the arms employed in his apostolic ministry.

*mighty to God,* that is, "*mighty in the sight of God*" or "*according to the measure by which God judges*"; though some commentators take it as meaning, "*mighty through the co-operation of God.*"

**4–6.** The metaphor contained in these verses is derived from the siege and capture of a rebellious city—pulling down the fortified walls by which error is protected; destroying every counsel of human wisdom which opposes the knowledge of the truth, and which is compared to the high towers upon the walls; and finally reducing all the inhabitants to submission, and after this is accomplished, punishing the leaders of the revolt.

**5.** *bringing into captivity,* that is, reducing every intellect and will to obedience.

**6.** *having in readiness . . .* It is evident that many of the Corinthians had been misled by the impostors, and St. Paul wishes to give them time to return to the obedience of Faith. But though he hopes that they will do this perfectly, yet he intimates that he is prepared when he comes to punish with excommunication any who remain obstinately disobedient.

**7.** *see the things . . .* that is to say, "*even from such outward appearances as these men take account of* (cf. *v.* 10) *you may see that I am a true minister of Christ.*" Their charges against his outward demeanour, if fairly examined, only showed his humility and their malice. The Greek can also be translated "*You see . . .*" or "*Do you see . . . ?*" If either of these translations be adopted, St. Paul is

If also I should boast somewhat more of our power, 8
which the Lord hath given us unto edification, and not
for your destruction ; I should not be ashamed. But that 9
I may not be thought as it were to terrify you by epistles,
(for his epistles indeed, say they, are weighty and strong ; 10
but his bodily presence is weak, and his speech contemptible,) let such a one think this, that such as we are 11
in word by epistles, when absent; such also *we will be*
in deed when present.
For we dare not match, or compare ourselves with some, 12

blaming those among the Corinthians who were willing to listen to
charges against him based on such merely external facts as his personal
appearance or manner of speech.
 *if any man* . . . These false teachers claimed that they, and the
original apostles of our Lord, with whom they presumed to couple themselves, were more truly the ministers of Christ than St. Paul, who had
not known our Lord during His earthly life (cf. xi. 5). To these St.
Paul says that if they will only consider the matter honestly in their
own minds, without any further evidence than what they have before
them, they will no longer be able to deny that he is the minister of
Christ as much as they are.
 **8.** *if also I should boast somewhat more.* St. Paul here suggests that
sufficient evidence to convince his adversaries, if they are sincere, is to
be found in the miraculous powers which God has given to him. The
meaning is, *If I were to go beyond putting myself on an equality with
these men* (as he appeared to do in the previous verse) *by magnifying
my powers above theirs, I could not be convicted of any exaggeration.*
 **9.** *but that I may not be thought* . . . The meaning is, *But I
refrain from making any such boast, that I may not lay myself open to
the charge which is brought against my letters, namely, that they are
written in strong language, and seem as if they were meant to frighten
the readers.*
 **10.** *his bodily presence.* According to tradition, St. Paul was short
in stature and of no imposing appearance (cf. Introduction chap. i.).
 *speech.* Cf. 1 Cor. ii. 1-5.
 **11.** *such as we are in word* . . . St. Paul here defends his consistency.
 *we will be.* These words are supplied in the English, not being
found in the Greek or Latin ; but it would probably be better to supply
the words "*we are*" : for the apostle is speaking rather of his habitual
conduct than of how he will behave on a particular occasion.
 **12-18.** These verses contain considerable difficulty, chiefly on
account of the various readings of the Greek MSS. The meaning of
v. 12 is apparently, " *We do not venture to count ourselves among or
rank ourselves with some of those* (false apostles) *who commend themselves ; but we are keeping ourselves within our own limits, and ranking
ourselves with ourselves.*"

that commend themselves: but we measure ourselves by ourselves, and compare ourselves with ourselves. But we will not glory beyond our measure; but according to the measure of the rule, which God hath measured to us, a measure to reach even unto you. For we stretch not out ourselves beyond our measure, as if we reached not unto you. For we are come as far as to you in the gospel of Christ. Not glorying beyond measure in other men's

*we dare not match* . . . This is either spoken ironically, or else it means, *we dare not associate ourselves with the presumption of those who claim an apostolate to which they have no title, and take to themselves credit for the work of others.*

*we measure ourselves by ourselves.* It appears from the way in which the same word is used in the following verses, that "*measure*" is to be taken here in the sense of "*limit.*" It means therefore "*we do not go outside those limits which God has appointed us,*" that is to say, he does not intrude his preaching into districts which have been assigned to other apostles, as these false teachers did.

*compare ourselves with ourselves.* He claims only that rank (namely, the rank of apostle), which God has given him. St. Paul intimates that he would have been as wrong if he had, out of weakness, neglected to vindicate his Divine authority, as his opponents were in claiming an authority to which they had no right, and asserting for themselves an equality with the original apostles of our Lord, or at least a commission from them which placed them above St. Paul.

According to the reading of the majority of extant Greek MSS. the last clause of this verse would run "*They measuring themselves by themselves and comparing themselves with themselves are not wise.*" This would mean that they measure themselves by their own standard instead of by that of God. But the intrinsic objections to this reading are that it does not fit in well with the context, and that it compels us to take the words "*measuring*" and "*comparing*" in a different sense from that in which they are used in the context. There can be little doubt therefore that the Vulgate translation represents the original of this verse.

**13.** *we will not glory beyond our measure* . . . that is, *we will not boast of anything we have done outside that sphere of work which God has commissioned us to undertake, but Achaia is included in that sphere.* Early tradition asserts that the apostles divided the world between them, each undertaking to preach in certain countries. St. Paul, who was especially the apostle of the Gentiles, was led by God to preach as far at least as the Grecian Peninsula.

**14.** *as if we reached not unto you.* St. Paul reached as far as Corinth both in the allotment of his sphere of labour, and in the fact that he was the first to preach and to found a Church there.

**15.** *having hope of your increasing faith* . . . that is, *having a hope that as your faith grows, our glory will be increased both among you, and* labours; but having hope of your increasing faith, to be magnified in you according to our rule abundantly. Yea, 16 unto those places that are beyond you, to preach the gospel, not to glory in another man's rule, in those things that are made ready to our hand. But he that glorieth, 17 let him glory in the Lord. For not he who commendeth 18 himself is approved, but he whom God commendeth.

## CHAPTER XI.

WOULD to God you could bear with some little of my folly: but do bear with me. For I am 2 jealous of you with the jealousy of God. For I have espoused you to one husband, that I may present you as a chaste virgin to Christ. But I fear lest, as the serpent 3

*also through your assistance and by means of your example, in the regions beyond you*, such, e.g., as Illyricum, where St. Paul hoped to form a Church.

**16.** *not to glory in another man's rule* . . . He did not wish to get glory by preaching in a place allotted to some other apostle, nor where some other had prepared the way by preaching before him.

**17.** *in the Lord*, that is, not taking the credit of his success to himself, but attributing it to our Lord.

**18.** *he who commendeth himself*, like these false teachers who praised themselves and claimed powers they did not possess.

*whom God commends*, by the works which He enables him to perform.

## CHAPTER XI.

**1.** *my folly*—i.e., that which he has just declared to be folly, namely, self-praise; which, however, is necessitated by the danger in which he sees them placed.

**2.** *I am jealous of you.* The reason why he is foolish, and why they should bear with his folly, is because it proceeds from a true love of God and of them, a love which brooks no rival.

*with the jealousy of God*, that is, his jealousy was not for his own sake, but for that of God, because these men were leading the Corinthians from the love of God. As he had espoused them to Him, he was jealous when he saw any man trying to make them unfaithful to their Spouse.

*a chaste virgin.* The singular number expresses the fact that all the faithful form one body, that is, one Church, which ought to be chaste in all its members.

**3.** *I fear* . . . St. Paul does not wish to offend and alienate his converts by any suggestion that they wished to be unfaithful, but he says he is afraid they may be misled and drawn into error by the craftiness

seduced Eve by his subtilty, so your minds should be corrupted, and fall from the simplicity that is in Christ.
4 For if he that cometh preacheth another Christ, whom we have not preached; or if you receive another Spirit, whom you have not received; or another gospel, which you have not received: you might well bear *with him*.
5 For I suppose that I have done nothing less than the

of the devil; and as Eve was beguiled by false promises, they may be led astray by similar deceptions, so as to fall from the pure affection towards our Lord, which is a characteristic of the true faith, into the confusion between God and the world, which is commonly a note of heresy.

*in Christ.* The Greek means "*to Christ*" (εἰς τὸν χριστόν). Many Greek MSS. insert "*and chastity*" after "*simplicity.*"

**4.** *he that cometh* perhaps refers to some special leader of the false teachers, but more probably denotes any one of them indefinitely. In either case it seems to be implied that these false teachers had no mission to Corinth, but came there without any authority: and that they certainly were not Corinthians. The meaning of the verse is, *If he preach some new truth, beyond what I taught, your tolerance of him is justified.* The language is ironical, because it was certain that the faith preached by St. Paul was the absolute truth, and therefore that the tolerance which some of the Corinthians displayed towards these false teachers was a compromise of principle.

*another Christ . . . another spirit . . . another gospel.* It is probable that the false teachers (like the Ebionites) perverted the truth of the Incarnation, claimed that they were the first to give the Holy Ghost to the Corinthians, and corrupted the true faith by an admixture of Judaism. However, for the present, St. Paul does not refer to the falsehood of their doctrine, but contents himself with an indirect appeal to the knowledge which the Corinthians had that the false apostles had nothing to add to the faith they had received from himself.

**5.** *the great apostles.* Some modern commentators have supposed that this phrase refers ironically to the false teachers, *those who consider themselves as very eminent apostles:* but this is opposed to the interpretation of all the Fathers, who unanimously regard it as referring to the true apostles, especially Sts. Peter, John, and James. The word "*great*" occurs again in xii. 11, and is there translated "*above measure.*" It is used here in reference to the exaggerated deference which the false teachers at Corinth professed to pay to what they represented as being the teaching of these apostles, as though they were apostles in some special sense, in which St. Paul could not claim comparison with them. The true meaning is seen by a reference to the circumstances. The false teachers professed to be the representatives of the original twelve apostles (especially of Sts. Peter, James, and John), whose doctrine they pretended was contrary to that of St. Paul. These apostles, (in order to depreciate St. Paul's authority,) they called the *great apostles*

great apostles. For although I be rude in speech, yet not 6
in knowledge: but in all things we have been made
manifest to you.

Or did I commit a fault, humbling myself, that you 7
might be exalted? Because I preached unto you the

St. Paul therefore says here (and in xii. 11) that he has the marks of a true apostle no less than those whom his opponents profess to represent. Some Protestant commentators have imagined that St. Paul is here denying the Primacy of St. Peter. But it is clear that the equality which he is claiming is an equality in knowledge of the Faith, in apostolic authority, and in the power of the Holy Ghost to work miracles and to propagate the gospel, in all of which things it is agreed that the apostles were on an equal footing; and which do not affect the Primacy of St. Peter. What St. Paul is rather attacking in this passage is the disposition, manifested by schismatics in all ages, to appeal from the voice of the Church speaking by its authorized ministers in their midst, to some more distant and inaccessible authority, whom they claim as favouring their own sect.

6. *although I be rude in speech.* This verse recurs to the charge brought against him (cf. x. 10) that his speech was not polished in accordance with the accepted rules of rhetoric. The word (ἰδιώτης) translated "*rude*" means *an amateur*, one who had had no professional training in oratory. We can see from his writings that his style was often obscure, and his Greek barbarous; but in spite of these defects his earnestness and God's grace made his letters forcible and eloquent.

*not in knowledge.* It is knowledge and not eloquence which is the true requisite of an apostle; and St. Paul here implies that his opponents who boasted of their rhetoric were deficient in the knowledge of the Faith.

*in all things we have been made manifest.* That is, either, *in all things we have dealt openly and candidly*, and not like the false apostles, appearing one thing and being another (cf. iv. 2), or *we have been shown by all our doings to be true apostles* (cf. xii. 12). Some Greek MSS. have "*in all things we have made it manifest,*" that is, we have shown our knowledge, and not kept it hidden.

7-12. It seems that the false teachers at Corinth maintained that St. Paul betrayed consciousness of his lack of authority by the fact that he asked no pay for his services. He is therefore obliged, for the glory of God and the honour of his apostolate, to expose the meanness of this charge, by showing that he forbore from this only to prevent the possibility of his being charged with venality (cf. 1 Cor. ix. 11, 12, &c.).

*did I commit a fault.* This is spoken in bitter irony against those who would make a fault out of his self-sacrifice.

*humbling myself,* by working for his living at tent-making (Acts xviii. 3), and appearing among them as a poor man; unlike his opponents (cf. *v.* 20).

8 gospel of God freely? I have taken from other churches,
9 receiving wages of them for your ministry. And, when I was present with you, and wanted, I was chargeable to no man: for that which was wanting to me, the brethren supplied who came from Macedonia: and in all things I have kept myself from being burthensome to you, and so
10 I will keep myself. The truth of Christ is in me, that this glorying shall not be broken off in me in the regions
11 of Achaia. Wherefore? Because I love you not? God
12 knoweth it. But what I do, that I will do, that I may

8. *I have taken from other churches.* The original is stronger, and means "*I have robbed*" or "*spoiled.*" By this verse he shows that he claimed the right of receiving pay from those to whom he ministered, and even from one region for the benefit of another.

*for your ministry,* i.e., to enable me to minister to you.

9. *the brethren . . . who came from Macedonia.* Cf. Acts xviii. 5. It appears from this that they brought him money contributed by the Macedonians. The meaning of the whole verse is apparently, *When I was with you, and my own labour did not supply sufficient for my needs, the deficiency was supplied, not by you, but by the contributions of the Macedonians.* The liberality of the Church of Philippi in particular is referred to in his Epistle to the Philippians (iv. 15).

*I will keep myself.* It seems that though St. Paul had accepted the contributions of the Macedonians, he would not ask for anything from the Corinthians for his own use; because the gifts of the former had been spontaneous and liberal (like their offerings for the poor of which he speaks in viii. 1–5); while it is evident that the charity of the latter was less ready.

10. *the truth of Christ is in me.* As Christ, who is the Truth, speaks in him (cf. xiii. 3), therefore what he says is true (cf. 1 Cor. ix. 15).

*this glorying,* namely, that he preaches for nothing, and abstains from lawful wealth for the sake of their salvation.

11. *because I love you not?* Apparently it was another insinuation of the heretics that St. Paul did not take their gifts because he had no affection for them, and wished to put himself under no obligation to them.

*God knoweth it,* that is, *God knows the truth about this charge,* namely, *that I do love you.* The true reason for his receiving no pay is explained in the following verse.

12. *what I do, that I will do.* . . . This verse is difficult, and has been explained in various ways. The simplest way of explaining it is: *I will continue to take no pay for my preaching, so as to cut off from my rivals the opportunity,* which they desire to have, of boasting against me of their disinterestedness: for if I preach freely myself, we shall be put on an equality in this respect. This is the explanation adopted by very

cut off the occasion from them that desire occasion, that wherein they glory, they may be found even as we. For many commentators, but there is this difficulty that it assumes that the false teachers received no pay, or at least that they received none openly, which appears to be in direct opposition to v. 20. Moreover, the false teachers, who claimed to be the representatives of the first apostles, would not be likely to forego the claim to a right which the latter exercised (cf. 1 Cor. ix. 12). But this interpretation is accepted by very many of the Fathers, and, in spite of its difficulties, seems on the whole the best, as it certainly is the most obvious, way of explaining the verse. If we adopt it, we may suppose, as some of the Fathers have suggested, that the false apostles, being richer than St. Paul, sought to win the worldly-minded by making a boast of preaching for nothing, but yet did receive gifts in secret ; so that St. Paul, in order to avoid the slightest possibility of scandal, wishes to make himself what they pretend to be (cf. Rom. xvi. 17, 18 ; Phil. iii. 17–19).

A second interpretation of the verse is : *I will continue to take no money, so as to cut off their opportunity of getting money* (namely, by alleging my example), *that as they boast* (untruly) *of being like us in taking no money, they may be found like us*, i.e., may be forced against their will really to resemble us, by getting nothing from you, either openly or secretly. This is open to the same objection that there is no evidence that they made any such boast ; it seems more probable from v. 20 and from 1 Cor. ix., that they accepted money openly.

A third interpretation depends on a different translation, namely, "*from them that desire occasion that they may be found like us (in which they glory)*." The meaning, then, is : *I will continue to preach freely so that those who desire to appear like us* (i.e., both receiving pay), *and who boast of being like us, may be cut off from such an appearance, and from the opportunity of such a boast.* The latter meaning seems in some respects to suit best the circumstances and the context, and is therefore adopted by many commentators. One objection to this explanation as well as to the preceding one, is that both of them make the false apostles claim, and boast of, an equality with St. Paul, whereas the essence of their opposition to him lay in the claim of superiority to him.

**13-15.** In these verses St. Paul continues to give the true character of these false apostles. He explains the reason why he wishes to cut off their ground of boasting, namely, that they are not really what they profess to be.

*false apostles*. The word *apostle* means *one sent*, a legate or messenger ; and therefore implies the position of authority from God which these men falsely claimed.

*deceitful*: either by pretending to take no money whilst they accept it in secret ; or else by pretending to be working for the spiritual good of the Corinthians, whilst they are really perverting the Faith and seeking their own glory.

such false apostles are deceitful workmen, transforming
14 themselves into the apostles of Christ. And no wonder:
for Satan himself transformeth himself into an angel of
15 light. Therefore it is no great thing if his ministers be
transformed as the ministers of justice: whose end shall
be according to their works.
16 Again I say, (let no man think me to be foolish, other-
17 wise take me as foolish, that I also may glory a little,) that
which I speak, I speak not according to God, but as it

*transforming themselves*, that is, trying to make themselves appear as true apostles; like the false teachers of whom St. Paul warned Timothy, "having an appearance of godliness" (2 Tim. iii. 5; cf. Matt. vii. 15).

**14.** *an angel of light.* The good angels are angels of light, that is, (as the next verse shows,) because they dwell in the eternal light of God, who is supreme Justice. Satan, before his fall, was known in heaven as Lucifer, the Light-bearer, but by falling from grace he has become the prince of the powers of darkness. But he still assumes the form of a good spirit, chiefly by presenting evil under the form of good. For he commences by inspiring good thoughts, but gradually draws the soul from these into things less good, so that he is known, as St. Ignatius says, "by his serpent's tail."

**15.** *ministers of justice.* The apostles are ministers of justice, and the false teachers tried to pass themselves off as such.

**16.** *again I say.* He now resumes what he had commenced to say in *v.* 1, when he was interrupted by the necessity of vindicating his love for them, and his disinterestedness.

*let no man . . .* This sentence is inserted as a parenthesis. He has already said (*v.* 1) that he is about to do a foolish thing, namely to commend himself. He does not do it out of foolishness, however, but under compulsion. Nevertheless he fears that the apparent folly of his boasting may form a reason, or an excuse, to some of them for refusing to hear him; and so, as he is more anxious to vindicate the Divine authority of his apostolate than his own wisdom, and has no object in view in his boasting but the glory of God, he says: *Even if you will not regard me otherwise than as a fool, yet, regarding me as a fool, receive me, and attend to what I have to say.* Thus he converts even the necessity for self-praise into an opportunity of practising humility.

*that I also . . .* These words contain a gentle irony. He asks the Corinthians who had endured so much of the self-commendation of their false teachers to allow him also, their true apostle, to glory in a small degree.

**17-19.** These verses give the reasons (1) why in general it is foolish to boast; (2) why in spite of this he does boast; (3) why they should bear with his boasting.

**17.** *I speak not according to God.* That is, what he says is not in

were in foolishness, in this matter of glorying. Seeing that 18
many glory according to the flesh, I will glory also. For 19
you gladly suffer the foolish : whereas yourselves are wise.
For you suffer if a man bring you into bondage, if a man 20
devour *you*, if a man take *from you*, if a man be lifted
up, if a man strike you on the face. I speak accord- 21
ing to dishonour, as if we had been weak in this part.

its matter after the mind and spirit of our Lord, who forbids boasting,
but the intention with which it is said is purely for God's glory.

**18.** *seeing that many glory according to the flesh* . . . The false
apostles boasted of things which St. Paul has now several times
called foolishness ; namely, such external things as Hebrew birth,
circumcision, having seen our Lord, wisdom, perhaps even wealth.
Why then does St. Paul not pass over these things as idle boasts, and
things of no account? The reason is, as St. Chrysostom says, that he
finds it necessary to speak " not to adorn himself, but to humble them."
For if he shows that he possesses all the qualifications of which they boast,
and at the same time makes it clear that he regards all these as mere
folly and worthlessness, then indeed he will leave his opponents without
out the least support for their pretensions. In this he is following the
advice of Solomon when he says " Answer a fool according to his folly,
lest he imagine himself to be wise " (Prov. xxvi. 5).

**19.** *you gladly suffer the foolish* . . . that is to say, *you ought in
reason to bear with me, because you always show yourselves very ready
to bear with fools, and indeed you seem to consider that you show your
own wisdom by doing so*. The verse is ironical, as the Corinthians
prided themselves on their wisdom (cf. 1 Cor. iv. 10 ; x. 15).

**20.** *if a man bring you into bondage*. Some writers suppose that
this means bondage to the Jewish law, which the false teachers tried to
impose on all Christians ; but the context seems to make it clear that
slavery to themselves is to be understood.

*devour you*, that is *devour your property* (cf. Matt. xxiii. 14).

*if a man take from you* (εἴ τις λαμβάνει). This may also be translated
" *if a man catch you* (as in xii. 16) *by deceit.*"

*if a man be lifted up* (εἴ τις ἐπαίρεται). This would be better translated " *if a man extols himself*," referring to these false teachers, who
regarded themselves as superior to the Corinthians because of their
Jewish descent.

*if a man strike you on the face*. There is some doubt whether these
words are to be taken literally. If they are so taken, they will show
the extremity of insult on the one side, and of forbearance on the other
(cf. Matt. v. 39; Luke xxii. 64 ; Acts xxiii. 2). But many commentators consider that the words are not to be taken literally, but are to be
explained by the following words : " *I speak according to dishonour*,"
that is, *I mean, if he should offer you the greatest insult.*

**21.** *I speak according to dishonour, as if we had been weak in this*

Wherein if any man dare (I speak foolishly) I dare also.
22 They are Hebrews: so am I. They are Israelites: so am I. They are the seed of Abraham: so am I.

*part.* (κατὰ ἀτιμίαν λέγω, ὡς ὅτι ἡμεῖς ἠσθενήκαμεν). This verse may be explained in various ways.

(1) If we do not take its first clause with the preceding verse, then it may be understood ironically, and be translated thus: "*I say to my own shame, that I have been weak in this respect*"; that is to say, inasmuch as it seems that you respect only the overbearing, I confess that I have acted in a manner which you must regard as weak and shameful in not imitating these men. Or it may be, "*I say it to your shame, as if we had been weak in this respect*": meaning that it is a disgrace to the Corinthians that they despise the meekness and charity of their true apostle, and attribute his conduct to weakness, while allowing themselves to be overridden by an impostor (cf. *v.* 7).

(2) If we take the first clause as explaining the previous verse the meaning will be either "*They enslave you, devour your substance, and insult you, just as if we had been weak,*" that is, they entirely disregard our authority in doing these things; or else, "*You bear with their usurpations, their exactions, their insolence; but you do not bear with me, you treat me as weak.*"

*wherein* . . . According to which interpretation of the previous clause we adopt, this must be taken either (1) as dropping the ironical mode of speech—*I say ironically that we have been weak, but in truth we are as bold as any man:* or (2) as contrasting the weakness which was imputed to him, whether by the Corinthians or by the false apostles, who insinuated that he had nothing to boast of, with the actual facts. Another way of taking the sentence is—"*In that matter in which any man is bold (I mean in foolishness), I am bold also*": which is equivalent to saying, *The matters of which my opponents boast are vain and foolish, nevertheless, even in these matters, I am not inferior to them.*

22. *Hebrews.* This word denotes the nationality of the Jews; the name "*Israelites*" indicates that they are the chosen people of God (cf. Rom. ix. 4); and the expression "*seed of Abraham*" shows them to be related to the Messiah, who was to arise, according to God's promise, amongst Abraham's descendants. Though St. Paul considers these matters of no importance in themselves, yet when he is compelled by his adversaries, he shows that in them all he is their equal. In the next verse he proceeds to show that in such matters as are of consequence, namely the Divine ministry, he is far above them: and this he proves, first, by his surpassing them in sufferings (*vv.* 23-33), and secondly, by the spiritual favours he has received from God (xii. 1-6, 12).

22, 23. It is open to doubt whether the four clauses commencing "*They are* . . ." in these two verses ought not to be taken as questions. If they are so taken, the meaning will be: "*Are they Hebrews,*" &c., that is: *Do they claim to be Jews and ministers of Christ?* Even if

They are the ministers of Christ: (I speak as one less 23
wise,) I am more: in many more labours, in prisons more
frequently, in stripes above measure, in deaths often. Of 24
the Jews five times did I receive forty *stripes*, save one.
Thrice was I beaten with rods, once I was stoned, thrice 25

*these claims be true, at any rate I am their equal in the first respect and
their superior in the ministry.* This translation appears to suit the
facts better; because St. Paul would not have allowed that these false
apostles were in any real sense the ministers of Christ. If we take
the sentence affirmatively, we must suppose that "*they are*" is in this
verse equivalent to "*they profess to be.*"

**23.** *less wise* (παραφρονῶν). The Greek is much stronger than the
English, and means, "*I speak as one out of his mind,*" that is to say,
*If you think me foolish* (cf. v. 16) *for boasting of equality with these
men, you will consider me as quite mad when I claim to be superior to
them.*

*more labours . . . more frequently . . . above measure.* Probably
the translation should be "*in labours very frequently, in prisons very
frequently, in stripes above measure.*" But if we translate by the com-
parative we should keep it throughout, and have "*in stripes more than
they.*" In this case it will appear that these schismatics had also undergone persecution from the heathen. If this were true, it would not be
without example in Church history. St. Cyprian, for instance, was
obliged to warn the Catholics of his day, not to be led by admiration of
the sufferings undergone by some heretics into imitation of their errors
(cf. also 1 Cor. xiii. 3). But it does not appear that the false apostles
of Corinth were of this kind, and it is not likely that they would have
stood the test of imprisonment.

*in prisons.* See note on vi. 5.

*deaths.* Cf. note on i. 10. Some of these dangers of death are
mentioned in Acts xiv. 5, 6, xvii. 5, 13.

**24.** *forty stripes, save one.* The Law commanded that the
stripes given to an offender were not to exceed the number of forty
(Deut. xxv. 1–3). In order to prevent this number being exceeded
through any error, the greatest sentence inflicted was always thirty-
nine stripes, of which thirteen were given on the breast, and thirteen
on each shoulder. The punishment was inflicted with a scourge
composed of six leathern thongs, four of calf skin and two of ass's
skin; and it was so severe as sometimes to result in death. None
of these scourgings are mentioned in the Acts of the Apostles.

**25.** *beaten with rods.* This was a peculiarly Roman punishment,
and one from which St. Paul as a Roman citizen was by law exempt.
The only recorded occasion of his undergoing it was at Philippi
(Acts xvi. 22).

*once I was stoned*, namely, by the mob at Lystra (Acts xiv. 18).

*shipwreck.* The only recorded shipwreck of St. Paul (Acts xxvii.)
was some years later than this time.

I suffered shipwreck; a night and a day I was in the depth
26 of the sea. In journeyings often, in perils of water, in perils of robbers, in perils from my own nation, in perils from the gentiles, in perils in the city, in perils in the wilderness, in perils in the sea, in perils from false brethren:
27 in labour and painfulness, in much watchings, in hunger and thirst, in fastings often, in cold and nakedness.
28 Besides those things which are without: my daily instance,

*in the depth of the sea*, that is, probably, preserved after shipwreck upon some plank or raft. Some fathers suppose that St. Paul passed a night and a day under the waters of the sea, and was preserved, like Jonas, by a miracle; but it seems probable that so great a prodigy would have been more clearly referred to.

We see from this and the preceding verses how many things St. Luke omits in the Acts of the Apostles.

**26, 27** consist chiefly of the enumeration of the perils incident to his journeys.

*perils of waters.* Probably in crossing rivers, which often become very dangerous through being suddenly swollen by the heavy rains of the East.

*robbers.* St. John is said to have been carried off by bandits in the neighbourhood of Ephesus.

*my own nation.* Cf. Acts ix. 23, 24, xiii. 50, xiv. 5, 18, xvii. 5, 13, xviii. 12.

*the gentiles.* Cf. Acts xiv. 5, xvi. 19, 22, xix. 23-34; 1 Cor. xv. 32.

*in the city*, e.g., Damascus, Jerusalem, Antioch in Pisidia, Iconium, Lystra, Philippi, Thessalonica, Berœa, Corinth, Ephesus (cf. the preceding references).

*false brethren* may mean (as in Gal. ii. 4) Judaizers; but more probably it denotes hypocritical converts.

**27.** *painfulness*, that is, weariness as the effect of his labours.

*watchings.* When they were in prison at Philippi, he and Silas were praying at midnight, and singing praise to God (Acts xvi. 25). On another occasion he spent the whole night in preaching preparatory to celebrating the Holy Eucharist (Acts xx. 7, 11: cf. also *v*. 31). From 2 Thess. iii. 8 we gather also that after spending his days in mission work, he sat up at night to earn his living by working at his trade.

*hunger and thirst.* Cf. 1. Cor. iv. 11; Phil. iv. 12.

*fastings* here (as in vi. 5, and wherever the word occurs in Scripture) means voluntary fasts, and so is distinguished from the hunger and thirst mentioned above, which were due to want of food and drink.

*cold and nakedness.* Cf. 1 Cor. iv. 11.

**28.** *besides those things that are without.* This means either, "*besides those things which have been omitted*": or, more probably: "*besides those trials which are external, there is my constant solicitude for the churches.*" In the first case this clause would be the conclusion

the solicitude for all the churches. Who is weak, and I 29
am not weak? Who is scandalized, and I am not on fire?
If I must needs glory, I will glory of the things that con- 30
cern my infirmity. The God and Father of our Lord 31
JESUS CHRIST, who is blessed for ever, knoweth that I lie

of the passage extending from v. 23 to v. 27; in the latter case it would
be introductory to v. 28, and should be preceded by a full-stop.

*my daily instance* (ἡ ἐπίστασίς μοι [or μου] ἡ καθ' ἡμέραν). Probably
this is in apposition to *solicitude*, and means, "*that which is the matter
of my daily care.*" Some commentators understand it to mean, "*the
daily tumult against me.*"

*all the churches.* The numerous Churches founded by St. Paul himself and by his disciples no doubt chiefly occupied his thoughts. But
his solicitude was not entirely confined to these, as we see from the fact
of his writing a letter to the Church of Rome, before he had even visited
that city. As the Apostle of the Gentiles, and, in a minor degree, co-
founder of the Roman See, he shared in a measure with St. Peter the
care of all Churches.

**29.** *who is weak* . . . In this verse St. Paul shows that his solicitude
for the Churches extended also to their individual members.

*weak.* This may mean weak in faith or in virtue, but it seems to
have (as in Rom. xiv. and 1 Cor. viii.) a special reference to the
*scrupulous.* There were some, for example, who would not eat certain
food, either because it might have been offered in sacrifice to an idol,
or because it was ceremonially unclean by the law of Moses. Though
these things were in themselves indifferent, yet St. Paul abstained from
them in the company of these *weak brethren* to avoid giving scandal,
according to the rule which he has laid down in his Epistle to the
Romans (xiv. 21). "It is good not to eat flesh, and not to drink
wine, nor anything whereby thy brother is offended, or scandalized,
or made weak" (cf. Rom. xiv. (all); 1 Cor. viii.; ix. 22).

*who is scandalized* . . . that is, *Who is led into sin by bad
example, and I do not burn with zeal for his recovery*, or, *with
indignation against the offender.*

**30.** *if I must needs glory.* . . . Some commentators take this
verse as prefatory to the statement in vv. 32, 33; but most consider
that it refers to all that he has said about himself.

*the things that concern my infirmity:* that is, *all the things that make
me appear weak*, namely, his persecutions and trials. He glories in
these, as a Lapide says, for three reasons: (1) Because in them the
power of God's grace is shown; (2) Because in these things he surpassed the false teachers; (3) Because they are the distinguishing mark
of a true apostle.

**31.** *God and Father.* See note on i. 2. It is best to take this
verse as confirming all that the apostle says, and not merely the
statement to which it is prefixed.

32 not. At Damascus the governor of the nation under Aretas the king, guarded the city of the Damascenes to 33 apprehend me: and through a window in a basket was I let down by the wall, and so escaped his hands.

## CHAPTER XII.

IF I must glory (it is not expedient indeed:) but I will come to the visions and revelations of the Lord.

**32, 33.** This incident is referred to in Acts ix. 23 25. It occurred after the visit to Arabia which followed St. Paul's conversion.

*Aretas* was king of Arabia Petrea, and it is not quite clear how he came to be ruler of Damascus, which was the capital of Syria, and which was usually governed directly by the Romans. He was father-in-law of Herod Antipas, and when the latter divorced his wife to marry Herodias (cf. Mark vi. 17, &c.), a war broke out between them in which Herod was defeated with great loss. Hereupon, as he was a favourite with Tiberius, Herod appealed to Rome for aid, and Vitellius, governor of Syria, was ordered to go to his assistance against Aretas. Before, however, Vitellius had commenced operations, Tiberius died (A.D. 37), and Vitellius suspended hostilities until he should receive instructions from Caligula. What followed upon this is not known with certainty; but as Vitellius had a quarrel with Antipas, and as Caligula banished the latter two years later, it is natural to suppose that Aretas, whom he had so greatly wronged, was received into the new Emperor's favour. In the year A.D. 38 Caligula granted the sovereignty of several districts in the neighbourhood of Syria to local princes, and it is very likely that he gave Damascus to Aretas at this time, especially as that city had previously been held by his father, Obodas. This supposition is supported by the fact that we have Damascene coins of Augustus and Tiberius, and also of Nero, but none of the intervening Emperors Caligula and Claudius. If Damascus was not granted at this time to Aretas, the alternative is to suppose that he had seized the city, and was holding it against the will of the Romans, which is a very unlikely hypothesis.

*governor of the nation* (ὁ ἐθνάρχης). This is the title of a subordinate governor.

**33.** *through a window . . . was I let down by the wall.* In Damascus, as in other old cities, houses are built upon the city wall. The traditional spot of St. Paul's escape is on the south side of the city.

## CHAPTER XII.

**1-10.** In the last verses of the previous chapter St. Paul has shown his superiority to the false apostles in the sufferings he has undergone.

I know a man in Christ above fourteen years ago, (whether 2 in the body, I know not, or out of the body, I know not, God knoweth,) such an one rapt even to the third heaven.

Now he proceeds to show how he surpasses them in the gifts he has received from God. These gifts are of two kinds: first, the visions and revelations which he has had from God (*vv.* 1-4), which he passes over and refuses to make the subject of glorying (*vv.* 5, 6); and secondly, those which he receives more willingly, namely, those which bring him no honour among men, but which preserve and increase his virtue (*vv.* 7-10).

1. *if I must glory.* The Greek MSS. of this verse exhibit considerable difference of reading. Most of them omit the word "*if*," and some read "*for*" in the place of "*but.*" A few also have the reading "*To glory* [*indeed*] *is not expedient* [*for me*]; *but* [or *for*] *I will come to the visions . . .*" It will be seen, however, that these variations do not materially affect the sense of the passage. The language of St. Paul is very abrupt, owing, no doubt, to the contradictory influences by which he was being moved; and this abruptness has probably misled the copyists, and caused them to attempt various emendations of the text. Omitting the word "*if*," it may be translated either "*I must glory,*" or "*Must I glory*"? The meaning is, *if*, for your sakes, *I am obliged to glory, it is not expedient*, that is, for myself. It may be that the word *indeed* is here inserted (as in x. 1) to denote an objection of his opponents: *They indeed will say that it is not expedient for me to boast.*

*visions and revelations.* Visions are not always revelations, because sometimes they are not understood by those to whom they are given; as, for example, the vision of Pharao (Gen. xli.), and of Nabuchodonosor (Dan. ii. 4.) But revelations such as were given to Daniel (cf. Dan. vii. 16), Ezechiel (xxxvii. 11), and other prophets, include an understanding of the mystery.

*of the Lord,* that is, of our Lord JESUS Christ.

2. *a man in Christ,* that is, a Christian man, united to Christ by baptism (cf. Rom. xvi. 7). It is evident from *v.* 7 that he is speaking of himself, but he uses the third person to express his unwillingness to boast.

*above fourteen years ago,* that is A.D. 42 or 43, probably when he was at Antioch (cf. Acts xi. 25), before the beginning of his missionary journeys. The fact that he had kept silence about this ecstasy for so long a time proves the sincerity of his unwillingness to boast of it.

*whether in the body or out of the body* (see Appendix II.)

*the third heaven.* Some of the Jews spoke of three heavens, namely, the sphere of the air and clouds, the sphere of the stars, and the abode of the just. If St. Paul is speaking of a locality, it is probable that he is following this Jewish division. If, however, his soul and body remained on earth (see App. II.), he must be speaking of the highest degree of ecstasy, without allusion to any definite place.

3 And I know such a man (whether in the body, or out of
4 the body, I cannot tell : God knoweth :) that he was
caught up into Paradise ; and heard secret words, which it
5 is not granted to man to utter. For such an one I will
glory ; but for myself I will glory nothing, but in my
6 infirmities. For though I should have a mind to glory, I
shall not be foolish : for I will say the truth. But I forbear,
lest any man should think of me above that which
he seeth in me, or anything he heareth from me.
7 And lest the greatness of the revelations should exalt me,

3. *I know such a man* . . . It has been questioned whether the vision described in vv. 3, 4, is not different from that described in v. 2 ; but the common opinion is that they are the same.

4. *Paradise*. The word only occurs twice elsewhere in the New Testament (namely, in St. Luke xxiii. 43 and Apoc. ii. 7), and is evidently used for the abode of the blessed. In the Old Testament it means a garden (e.g., Cant. iv. 13), and it is used by the Septuagint translators to denote the Garden of Eden.

*heard secret words*, that is "*unutterable words.*" He did not hear them with his ears (for in that case he could not have doubted that he was in the body), but heavenly mysteries were imparted to his understanding without the intervention of his senses.

*which it is not granted to man to utter.* If St. Paul did not actually enjoy the beatific vision, as some commentators hold, at least he saw divine things after a supernatural manner, which human language cannot express.

5. *for such an one I will glory* . . . The meaning is, *I will glory for such a man* (that is for myself), *but not*, as might be supposed, on account of the visions already mentioned, but only on account of my sufferings and weakness through which God is glorified.

6. *though I should have a mind to glory* . . . The meaning here is : *If I did boast of these revelations, I should not be guilty of the folly of vain glory and untruth, for everything would be true. Nevertheless, I will say no more about these revelations, lest any man should think of me beyond what I deserve.* That is, although he might with truth praise himself, humility leads him to avoid the risk of giving any one too high an opinion of him.

*above that which he seeth in me* . . . This implies that what is apparent of St. Paul's actions and words will suffice for the necessary duty of vindicating his apostolate, without the addition of any self-praise (cf. x. 7).

7. *exalt me*, that is, *cause me to fall into pride*.

*a sting of my flesh*, that is, probably, temptation in the flesh. See Appendix III.

*was given me*. It was given by God, as is evident from the fact that there was given me a sting of my flesh, an angel of Satan to buffet me. For which thing thrice I besought the Lord, that it might depart from me: and he said to me: My grace is sufficient for thee: for power is made perfect in infirmity. Gladly therefore will I glory in my infirmities, that the power of Christ may dwell in me. For which cause I please myself in my infirmities, in reproaches, in necessities, in persecutions, in distresses, for Christ. For when I am weak, then am I powerful.

it was given for a good purpose (namely, to preserve St. Paul in humility). Yet it did not come immediately from God, who does not tempt men, but from the devil, whom God allowed to tempt the apostle for his greater sanctification and God's greater glory.

**8.** *thrice I besought the Lord.* That is to say, he prayed on three special occasions before our Lord gave him an answer; or it may be that the word *thrice* is used indefinitely to mean *often*.

*the Lord.* This means, according to the usage of St. Paul, not God the Father, but our Lord JESUS CHRIST.

**9.** *My grace is sufficient for thee.* Our Lord answered the prayer of St. Paul, not indeed by removing his temptation, but by giving him an assurance that he would have the grace to resist it without offending God by sin. St. Thomas says that our Lord gave St. Paul, not that which he asked, but that which he would have asked, if the purposes of God had been more fully revealed to him.

*power is made perfect in infirmity.* The power of God's grace has its perfect working in human weakness, because this weakness compels man to mistrust his own powers, and by casting himself entirely upon God, gain fresh grace. Consequently the holiness of the saints, which is the power of God working in them, is increased by temptation courageously withstood.

*gladly therefore will I glory in my infirmities.* The Greek inserts "*rather*," that is, *I will glory rather in my infirmities than in my visions and revelations* (vv. 5, 6); or else, *I will rather glory in my infirmities which display God's power*, than pray for their removal.

*that the power of Christ may dwell in me.* He glories in his temptations, because with the temptations he receives greater graces and a closer union with our Lord.

**10.** *I please myself*, that is, *I take pleasure*.

*infirmities.* It seems that in this word St. Paul refers to the subject of the preceding verses, while in those which follow he alludes to other sufferings undergone for Christ's sake.

*in necessities . . . in distresses.* See notes on vi. 4.

*then am I powerful*, that is, by the power of God working in him (cf. note on *v.* 9).

11 I am become foolish: you have compelled me. For I ought to have been commended by you: for I have no way come short of them that are above measure apostles: 12 although I be nothing. Yet the signs of my apostleship have been wrought on you in all patience, in signs, and 13 wonders, and mighty deeds. For what is there that you have had less than the other churches; but that I myself was not burthensome to you? Pardon me this injury.

11-13. Having finished his self-defence, St. Paul now again excuses himself for making it, by showing its necessity.

11. *I am become foolish.* This may be taken either as St. Paul's own statement, in which case it means, *I have acted in a manner which is usually a sign of folly;* or he may be alluding to an accusation which might be, or which actually had been, brought against him; either, *you will say I am become foolish*, or, *my opponents charge me with having become foolish* (viz., in self-praise).

*you have compelled me*—that is, though it is never wise in itself to boast, yet under the circumstances it was necessary to do so, for the sake of the Corinthians (cf. note on v. 1), especially as they, instead of vindicating him from his opponents, had rather listened to their slanders.

*them that are above measure apostles.* This phrase in the Greek is the same as that in xi. 5 (see note there), and refers to the apostles Peter, John, and James, the Bishop of Jerusalem.

*although I be nothing.* St. Paul means that of himself he is nothing, because all the power of his apostolate is to be attributed to the grace of Christ.

12. *yet the signs of my apostleship have been wrought on you . . .* This verse explains how, though St. Paul was in himself *nothing*, yet he possessed the notes of a true apostle, *in no way coming short of* the other apostles.

*in all patience:* is not parallel with *in signs*, &c., but qualifies *wrought*. It is the true mark of an apostle of Christ, not merely to work miracles of nature and of grace, but to do so with patience, not being affected by any opposition, but seeking only the glory of God.

*in signs, and wonders, and mighty deeds.* These are three different expressions to denote miracles.

13. *what is there that you have had less than the other churches?* The *other Churches* here referred to cannot be those founded by St. Paul himself, because the comparison is not between St. Paul's treatment of the Corinthians and his treatment of other Churches, but between his authority and that of other persons. He therefore compares the Church of Corinth, founded by himself, with Churches founded by those others with whom he is comparing himself, and whom in v. 11 he has called "those that are above measure apostles." It is clear from this verse that these are not, as some have supposed, the false apostles at Corinth (cf. note on xi. 5), because there is not the

Behold, now the third time I am ready to come to you; and I will not be burthensome unto you. For I seek not the things that are yours, but you. For neither ought the children to lay up for the parents, but the parents for the children. But I most gladly will spend and be spent myself for your souls: although, loving you more, I be loved less.

But be it so: I did not burthen you: but being crafty, 16

slightest reason to suppose that they ever founded any Churches. Moreover, if St. Paul had been comparing himself with these men, it would have been much simpler (instead of referring them to other Churches of which they would have less knowledge) to say: "What is there that you have had less from me than from them?"

*but that I myself was not burthensome to you.* He here refers again to the subject of xi. 7–12. What he says contains a severe rebuke of their want of generosity, and yet he expresses it in a form of apology which can offend no one. "He spoke thus," says St. Chrysostom, "at once to wound and to heal.... For this is wisdom's part, at once to lance, and to bind up the sore."

14. *the third time I am ready to come.* See Appendix I.

*I will not be burthensome unto you.* St. Paul adds this to show that his rebuke in the last verse was not intended to drive them to give unwillingly. So far from that, he is not hindered from coming again to them because he has received nothing in the past; and when he does come, he will refuse to take anything. And lest some of them should be grieved at this, as implying a want of confidence in their generosity, he proceeds to give two reasons for it.

*I seek not the things that are yours, but you.* That is, *I desire only your salvation, and not your temporal goods.*

*for neither ought . . .* He strengthens what he has said by a comparison with the law of nature, in which it is the duty of parents to provide the necessaries of life for their children, but children are not under the same obligation towards their parents. So St. Paul says that he has followed this example by providing the Corinthians with spiritual gifts, whilst taking no money from them. But the analogy does not apply if strictly pressed; for spiritual superiors have the right of receiving the necessaries of life from their spiritual children, as St. Paul had himself written to the Corinthians: "The Lord ordained that they who preach the gospel should live by the gospel" (1 Cor. ix. 14; cf. *vv.* 7–18).

15. *I most gladly will spend and be spent myself.* That is: *I will give you all that I have without asking anything in return, and I will give you also myself, devoting my life and my death to your salvation, and that not for any human motive, such as to win your love, but I will do all this for the love of God, even if I get no love from you in return.*

16. *but be it so . . .* This verse quotes a more subtle form which

17 I caught you by guile. Did I overreach you by any of
18 them whom I sent to you? I desired Titus, and I sent
with him a brother. Did Titus overreach you? Did we
not walk with the same spirit? did we not in the same
steps?
19 Of old, think you that we excuse ourselves to you?
We speak before God in Christ: but all things (my dearly
20 beloved) for your edification. For I fear lest perhaps
when I come, I shall not find you such as I would, and
that I shall be found by you such as you would not.
Lest perhaps contentions, envyings, animosities, dissensions, detractions, whisperings, swellings, seditions, be

the accusation against him took. His opponents, when it was clearly impossible to convict St. Paul of motives openly mercenary, said: *Well, be it so, let that charge be passed over; but at least he has overreached you by his craft and guile, by means of his agents.* It is this charge that he meets in the following verses, by appealing to their own knowledge of the facts.

**18.** *I desired Titus*, that is, I requested him to visit you. This visit of Titus is the one referred to in ii. 13, vii. 6, 13-15. He had returned from Corinth just before St. Paul wrote this Epistle.

*a brother*, that is, another Christian, sent as companion to Titus. Nothing else is known about him.

**19.** *of old, think you that we excuse ourselves to you?* St. Paul here resumes the main thread of his defence which was interrupted in *v.* 13. The meaning of this verse is: *Have you been supposing all this time* (i.e., while reading this letter) *that I have merely been writing to excuse myself? No, I declare to you in the presence of God, and in the spirit of Christ, I have not been considering my own defence, but your spiritual profit* (cf. 1 Cor. iv. 3).

**20.** *for I fear lest . . . I shall not find you such as I would. . . .* This verse explains the preceding by showing why it was necessary for the edification of the Corinthians that St. Paul should vindicate his authority, namely, lest he should find them impenitent when he came.

*such as I would.* This is explained by the last half of the verse.

*such as you would not.* The principal reference of this is explained in xiii. 2. It means that he will come with a severity which, if they are not truly penitent, they will dislike. There is, however, another reference in his words at which he charitably hints in *v.* 21, namely, that they will be pained at the sorrow which their sins cause him.

*detractions*, i.e., open slanders.

*whisperings*, i.e., secret slanders.

*swellings*, i.e., pride.

among you. Lest again, when I come, God humble me among you: and I mourn many of them that sinned before, and have not done penance for the uncleanness and fornication and lasciviousness, that they have committed.

## CHAPTER XIII.

BEHOLD, this is the third time I am coming to you. In the mouth of two or three witnesses shall every word stand. I have told before, and foretell, as present and now absent, to them that sinned before and to all the rest, that if I come again, I will not spare. Do you seek

**21.** *lest . . . God humble me*, i.e., by the apparent failure of his work at Corinth.
*I mourn*, over the loss to their souls.
*have not done penance.* The Greek word for penance denotes the change of will which is the chief part of contrition. In this passage the reference is probably to the works of penance quite as much as to contrition.

### CHAPTER XIII.

**1.** *the third time :* see Appendix I.
*in the mouth of two or three witnesses.* These words are quoted from the Jewish law as given in Deut. xix. 15, which enjoined that no man could be condemned unless there were at least two witnesses against him (cf. Matt. xviii. 16, xxvi. 59-61; John viii. 17, 18; 1 John v. 7, 8). It may be that St. Paul means to intimate that he will hold a regular investigation into the scandals when he arrives at Corinth, and condemn those against whom there is the evidence of two or three witnesses. But there is no indication of this in the context, and therefore many commentators have supposed that St. Paul means that his *visits* will be the witnesses. If those whom he has already found in sin once or twice on former occasions are still obstinately impenitent when he comes again, then this third visit will complete the evidence requisite to convict them.
**2.** *as present and now absent.* The Greek has: "*as present the second time, and now absent*" (see Appendix I). Following the hypothesis that St. Paul had already visited Corinth twice, the meaning of this verse is: *I have foretold you, and I do now foretell you, as I did when present with you the second time, and I do now when absent.*
*to them that sinned before, and to all the rest.* That is to those mentioned in xii. 21 who had sinned previously to his last visit, and to any others who had fallen into sin since that time.
**3.** *do you seek a proof of Christ that speaketh in me . . . ?* These

a proof of Christ that speaketh in me, who towards you is
4 not weak, but is mighty in you? For although he was
crucified through weakness; yet he liveth by the power of
God. For we also are weak in him; but we shall live with
5 him by the power of God towards you. Try your own selves

words, taken in accordance with the Greek, may refer back to v. 2, meaning: *as you seek a proof . . . I tell you that . . . I will not spare*. But more probably they relate to what follows, and the meaning is: *As you wish to prove that Christ dwells in me and speaks in me, and you mock me as if destitute of His power* (x. 10): *you shall have sufficient proof of my severity, if you force me to it* (cf. vv. 5, 6, 7, and notes).

*is mighty in you;* that is, Christ who speaks by St. Paul, works powerfully in the Corinthian Church, both by the miracles which St. Paul performed by His power, and by the punishments he was enabled to inflict (cf. xii. 12; and 1 Cor. v. 4, 5).

4. *although he was crucified through weakness . . .* St. Paul says in this verse that though he may appear weak when he suffers persecution, &c., just as our Lord, through the weakness of the human nature which He had assumed, underwent infamy and death, veiling for a time His Divinity; yet as Christ suffered no real loss of power, but restored Himself to life by His Divine might, so by the same Divine power dwelling in him, His apostle will live and have power to punish all offenders against God.

*although.* This word is omitted in the best Greek MSS.

*through weakness.* That it might be possible for our Lord to be put to death it was necessary for Him, in the first place, to join to His Divine nature a human nature which should be capable of suffering and of death, and secondly, to refrain during His Passion from the operations of His Divinity, so as to leave the humanity unsupported and so able to die. These two facts make it possible to say that He was crucified through weakness (cf. 1 Cor. i. 25).

*by the power of God.* Our Lord was raised to life and lives through the power of God the Father, which is one with His own power.

*we also are weak in him.* Cf. iv. 10, 11, and notes.

*we shall live with him . . .* i.e., *as we are partakers of His sufferings, so we shall be of His power and glory. The same Divine Power which raised Him, will raise us up, and give us power to judge you.* St. Paul's sufferings are a sign of his union with our Lord, and this union is the source of his strength.

5. *Try your ownselves if you be in the faith; prove ye yourselves.* There are two ways in which this verse may be taken:—

(1) It may be an answer to the question in v. 3, in which case it will mean: [*If you require such a proof,*] *consider merely your own selves, and you will find among yourselves the proof* [*that I have preached among you the true Gospel by the authority of God*]. *For you know that*

if you be in the faith: prove ye yourselves. Know you not your own selves, that CHRIST JESUS is in you, unless perhaps you be reprobates? But I trust that you shall

[*since you were converted by my preaching,*] *the power of Christ has been working among you,* [*by the effects both of grace and of miracles:*] *unless indeed this evidence of God's power has been forfeited by your fault.* If this be the true meaning of the verse, the implied argument is that the grace of miracles, which is given by God usually in order to attest the truth of doctrine, would not have followed St. Paul's teaching, unless he had been a duly accredited apostle. This is the meaning which is given to the verse by the great majority of commentators, and the one which seems best adapted to the context.

(2) A different explanation, however, has sometimes been put forward, namely, that St. Paul is warning the Corinthians against pressing him to give an exhibition of that power which they wish to prove. If so, the meaning will be: [*Instead of compelling me to prove Christ's co-operation with me,*] *prove your own selves, examine your consciences, see whether you are leading faithful lives. For you know that the grace of Christ dwells in you, unless, indeed, you have fallen into a state which will not stand this proof.* Though this explanation is supported by less authority than the other, it nevertheless makes good sense, and it has this fact in its favour, that the word *prove* is used here with a meaning analogous to that in other passages of St. Paul's writings, namely, of the examination of one work and conscience in the light of known truth. Cf. Gal. vi. 4: "Let every man prove his work"; and 1 Cor. xi. 28: "Let a man prove himself, and so let him eat of that bread," &c.

*in the faith.* If the first of the above explanations be adopted, this expression may be taken to mean either of two things:—

(*a*) the true faith objectively considered. In this case the meaning will be: *Consider whether you have not received the true faith. For you know that the miracles of nature and of grace wrought amongst you by the power of Christ attest it.*

(*b*) The faith which works miracles. The meaning will then be: *Consider whether you have amongst you faith to work miracles. For you know that our Lord is working such miracles in your midst.*

If, on the other hand, the second explanation of the verse were adopted, then the words "in the faith" would refer to that faith which works by charity.

*reprobates* (ἀδόκιμοι). This word is not here used in its usual theological sense, denoting those who are doomed to damnation. The meaning is, *unless you have become unable to stand the proof,* either by losing the grace of miracles, or by moral corruption. With regard to miraculous powers, it must be remembered that they were very common in the early Church, when the faith was new and needed attestation before the world.

6. *I trust that you shall know that we are not reprobates.* That is to say: *however it may be with you, I hope to let you know that I have*

7 know that we are not reprobates. Now we pray God that you may do no evil, not that we may appear approved, but that you may do that which is good, and that we may be
8 as reprobates. For we can do nothing against the truth,
9 but for the truth. For we rejoice that we are weak, and you are strong. This also we pray for, your perfection.
10 Therefore I write these things being absent, that, being present, I may not deal more severely, according to the power which the Lord hath given me unto edification, and not unto destruction.

11 For the rest, brethren, rejoice, be perfect, take exhorta-

*not become incapable of standing the proof to which you will put me, if you force me to use the power given me by God, in punishing you.*

7–9. St. Paul explains in these verses how unwilling he is to punish, saying that he would rather appear destitute of the power of God, than that they should sin, and so force him to exercise this power.

*not that we may appear approved,* that is, we do not pray for anything other than your reformation, even though thereby our apostolic power, and the presence of God with us, might be vindicated.

*as reprobates,* that is, *as if deprived of the power of inflicting divine punishments.* This would be the consequence of their amendment for two reasons; first, because he would then have no occasion to punish them; and secondly, as he explains in the next verse, because, even if he should wish to do so, he would not be able to punish them, but if he were to attempt it, God would not work with him.

8. *we can do nothing against the truth.* That is, *we have no power given us by God to inflict a punishment contrary to the truths of the facts.*

9. *we rejoice that we are weak.* The Greek has, "*We rejoice when we are weak . . .*" The meaning is that explained above: "*We are glad when you are strong in virtue, and we are consequently weak in the power of punishing you.*"

*this also we pray for, your perfection.* He concludes by saying that all his desire is for their continual growth in virtue. He prays for nothing short of their perfection.

10. *therefore I write these things being absent.* This verse explains the severity of the letter. If he has been obliged to write sternly it has been that they may repent, and so prevent him using his power when he comes. And at the same time he explains that if this power were used at any time it would only be used for their good, to build up, and not to destroy, spiritual graces in them.

11–13. Conclusion of the whole epistle. St. Paul addresses those who have not sinned, and even those who have sinned, as trusting that they are now penitent.

tion, be of one mind, have peace: and the God of peace and of love shall be with you.

Salute one another in a holy kiss. 12
All the saints salute you.
The grace of our Lord JESUS CHRIST, and the charity 13 of God, and the communication of the Holy Ghost be with you all. Amen.

**11.** *rejoice.* To rejoice in those things which you do to the service of God is necessary, St. Thomas says, in order to be virtuous and just. It is necessary always to have joy in the service of God, because no one continues long in that which causes him sadness.

*be perfect*, that is, *continually strive towards perfection.*

*take exhortation*, or *consolation* (see i. 3-6 and notes).

*be of one mind*, by having the same faith and loving the same object.

*have peace.* This is the outward result of being of one mind.

*the God of peace and of love shall be with you.* That is to say, *God, who is the author of peace and of love, will abide with you by more abundant gifts of grace.*

**12.** *salute one another in a holy kiss.* It was the custom in the early church during the Mass and before the Communion for a kiss to be given with the words "Pax tecum." This gave place to the kissing of a tablet, which is still preserved in monasteries, and other places; but in other churches it is represented only by an embrace, and this is confined to the clerics.

*all the saints.* That is, all the faithful who were with St. Paul.

**13.** All commentators have noticed that this verse contains a reference to all three Persons of the Blessed Trinity.

*the grace of our Lord* is the means of our justification and salvation.

*the charity of God* (cf. 1 John iv. 7-21). The charity of God the Father towards us, sent into the world His Son for our salvation; and by abiding in charity we are united to God, a union which is necessary for our salvation.

*the communication of the Holy Ghost* makes us possess the grace of salvation.

*amen.* This word is omitted by most Greek MSS.

# APPENDICES.

## APPENDIX I.

### VISITS OF ST. PAUL TO CORINTH.

" I had a mind to come to you before, that you might have a *second* grace: and to pass by you into Macedonia, and again from Macedonia to come to you" (i. 15, 16).

" I determined this with myself, not to come to you *again* in sorrow" (ii. 1).

" Behold, now *the third time* I am ready to come to you" (xii. 14).

" Behold, this is *the third time* I am coming to you. In the mouth of two or three witnesses shall every word stand. I have told before, and foretell, *as present* and now absent, to them that sinned before and to all the rest, that if I come again, I will not spare" (xiii. 1, 2).

These passages have given rise to the question whether St. Paul had not paid some visit to Corinth which is not related in Scripture. His only recorded visit previous to this date was on the occasion of his founding the Church of Corinth (Acts xviii.), and was therefore evidently his first one. It is evident that this visit was not made *in sorrow*, and there is no reason to suppose that when he was then *present* with them he threatened severity. If it be assumed that this was the only visit which St. Paul had as yet paid to Corinth the above passages may be explained in the following way. The *second grace* may be the visit he is about to make; the first grace being either their conversion, or perhaps the Epistles sent to them; but more probably the double grace will be the intended two visits, though the first of them was in fact never made. The word *again* may be considered as qualifying only the verb *come*, and not *in sorrow*; so that St. Paul will mean that he had determined that his second visit should not be a sorrowful one; and that he had therefore postponed it until, by their repentance, it could be made with joy. The number (*the third time*) in xii. 14, and xiii. 1, must be understood as spoken of visits intended, not of those actually made. And finally we must translate xiii. 2 (ὡς παρὼν τὸ δεύτερον καὶ ἀπὼν νῦν) by "as if I were present for the second time, though I am now absent." Several of these explanations, especially those of xiii. 1, 2, seem rather unnatural. Nevertheless they make good sense, and involve nothing impossible, and are supported by many authorities.

The alternative is to suppose that St. Paul had made some unrecorded visit to Corinth between the date of Acts xviii. and the time of writing this Epistle. It has been seen (cf. notes on xi. 24, &c.) how incomplete is the record in the Acts of St. Paul's travels. If such a visit was made it would probably have been during his stay of more than two years at Ephesus (Acts xix.). If this view be correct it will follow (from ii. 1 and xiii. 2) that this visit was one made in sorrow caused by the news of the disorders at Corinth, and that he threatened them with severity if he found them unreformed on his next visit. This visit would form the first grace, to which the intended visit of i. 15 was to have formed the second. This latter explanation seems to be decidedly the simpler of the two, and it derives some additional support from the words in xii. 14 (*I will not be burthensome unto you*), which seem to imply, *I will not be burthensome on this occasion, any more than on my previous visits.*

## APPENDIX II.

### THE ECSTASY OF ST. PAUL.

"whether in the body, I know not, or out of the body, I know not ; God knoweth " (xii. 2).

"whether in the body or out of the body, I cannot tell ; God knoweth" (xii. 3).

There is some question as to what are the two conditions with respect to which St. Paul wishes to express his doubt. Some suppose that the doubt lies between whether he was carried to heaven both body and soul, or whether his soul, leaving the body, was transported thither. Others consider that the doubt is whether the soul was transported to heaven without the body, or whether the soul, remaining in the body and upon earth, was miraculously enabled to see and to hear what was being done in heaven.

It is the most common opinion that St. Paul could not have been ignorant as to whether he was carried to heaven in body and soul, or in soul alone, because in the former case he would have seen and heard these mysteries with his bodily senses, and in the latter case, only in a supernatural manner. Moreover it appears most probable that the soul of the apostle was not separated from his body, because he would then have been dead, and another miracle would have been required to bring him to life again, and it is not becoming to suppose either that Almighty God would deprive a man of life in order to impart to him a revelation, or that He would multiply miracles without occasion. The alternative which remains is that which St. Thomas considers as the most probable, namely, that neither body nor soul was locally transported from the earth, but that the soul remaining in union with the body, in a supernatural state, saw and heard in a spiritual manner, apart from the bodily senses, the mysteries revealed by God. This view, though it cannot be regarded as certain, agrees best with what we know of the ecstasies of saints. Against it, however, two objections are brought. The first is, that the expression *rapt*, or *caught up*, implies an actual local motion: to which it may be replied that it may mean only an elevation of spirit above the things of sense. The second objection is, that such an actual bodily transportation into the presence of God was fitting in order to place him on an equality with the other apostles who had seen our Lord in the flesh; but this objection loses its force when it is remembered that St. Paul had seen our Lord (apart from this revelation) both at the time of his conversion (Acts ix. 17, xxii. 14, xxvi. 16; 1 Cor. xv. 8), and on other occasions (Acts xxii. 18).

## APPENDIX III.

### THE "STING OF THE FLESH."

" Lest the greatness of the revelations should exalt me, there was given me a sting of my flesh, an angel of Satan to buffet me " (xii. 7).

The question of what St. Paul here alludes to has given rise to much discussion. The translation offers little difficulty. The words *a sting of my flesh* are in Greek σκόλοψ τῇ σαρκί, that is, *a stake* (or *thorn*) *to* (or *in*) *my flesh*. The word *to buffet* is in the present tense (ἵνα με κολαφίζῃ), and therefore denotes that its effects were still continuing.

Of the various suppositions with respect to its nature, two may be dismissed at once.

1. It was not any sin, because it is implied that it was given him by God to preserve his humility, and because God refused to listen to his prayer for its removal.

2. It was not the recollection of sin, because in that case we cannot suppose that St. Paul would have prayed that it should cease.

These two quite impossible suppositions would not have been mentioned unless they had found supporters among modern Protestant commentators.

There are four other possible interpretations.

3. The reference may be to actual bodily attacks of devils, such as have befallen some saints, beating him and leaving his body wounded as if by thorns. This will suit the context, but it is supported by no tradition, and it is not likely that St. Paul would have asked to be delivered from it.

4. St. Chrysostom and other ancient commentators suppose that persecutions, or perhaps some particular opponent, are meant. This interpretation is supported by xi. 15, where the opponents of the apostle are called ministers of Satan, and to some extent by v. 10 of this chapter. But on the other hand such opposition or persecution is not very fittingly described as *in the flesh*, and it might well be rather a cause of glorying than of humiliation (cf. Matt. v. 12).

5. Others have supposed that it was some kind of bodily ailment. This receives some support from the fact that Tertullian and St. Jerome refer to a tradition that St. Paul suffered from a pain in the head or ears, but both of them only mention it as doubtful. Many other diseases or bodily defects have been suggested by other commentators, who support their theory by supposing that the allusion here is to the same thing as that mentioned in Gal. iv. 13, 14. They suppose that St. Paul means to state in the latter passage that he was detained in Galatia by some illness, which either disfigured him or in some way made him seem contemptible, and so might have given the Galatians occasion to despise him. The commonest conjecture of those who suppose an illness to be alluded to, is that it was either some nervous disease or acute ophthalmia, such as is prevalent in the East. Either of these might cause a great disfigurement, sufficient to tempt the Galatians to despise him. Moreover, either of these complaints might be the permanent result of the apostle's visions. It is a fact that his first vision at the time of his conversion resulted in a three days' blindness, and this may have been followed by a permanent affection of the eyes. Moreover, ophthalmia is nowhere more common than at Damascus, where St. Paul spent a considerable time after his conversion. There are also some passages of Scripture which seem to bear out this opinion, e.g., his failure to recognize the high priest (Acts xxiii. 5); and the passage in which he speaks of his own handwriting (according to many translators) as being written *in large characters* (πηλίκοις γράμμασιν ἔγραψα τῇ ἐμῇ χειρί. Gal. vi. 11).

But there is much to be said in opposition both to these arguments and to the opinion which they support. There is no evidence that St. Paul is here alluding to the same thing as in the Epistle to the Galatians. The latter passage, moreover, is understood by many in an entirely different sense, referring the *infirmity of the flesh* to the Galatians instead of to the apostle. It is impossible to suppose that, if he suffered from any disease which could make him loathsome to those who saw him, he could have been worshipped by the inhabitants of Lystra as Mercury, one of the most beautiful of all the heathen gods. The traditional accounts of his appearance, though they do not represent him as handsome, agree in regarding him as free from any disfigurement of this kind. The parallel passages cited prove, at the most, no more than that his sight was defective, which is a very different thing from his suffering from ophthalmia as it exists in the East, and one of which he could not have spoken in terms so strong as are here used. There is no other passage, among all those in which he mentions his sufferings, in which St. Paul refers to any chronic ailment. St. Chrysostom considers it impossible that one who had power to deliver over another to be punished by Satan with bodily illness (1 Cor. v. 5) should himself have been subject to the same infliction. Finally, the large variety of illnesses that has been suggested shows the difficulty of establishing any one, and the arguments brought forward in their support often mutually destroy one another. We conclude that, while a small defect of health would not have been mentioned so prominently, nor have led him to pray for deliverance, a serious illness, such as would have formed a grave obstacle to his missionary work, would in all probability have found a place in his own accounts of his sufferings, if not also in the narrative of St. Luke in the Acts.

6. We now come to the last supposition, which is adopted by the almost unanimous consent of modern Catholic commentators, namely that the *stake for the flesh* denotes temptations of concupiscence. This opinion derives support from Rom. vii. 23 and 1 Cor. ix. 27. St. Jerome and St. Gregory maintain it clearly, and also St. Augustine in a somewhat ambiguous passage, and in later times it has been adopted by St. Bede, St. Anselm, St. Thomas, and almost all more recent writers. There is nothing which would be more fittingly described as a *stake in the flesh*. There is nothing else from which St. Paul would be so sure to pray rather for deliverance than for strength to bear it. This was given him to preserve his humility, to keep him between presumption and despair; but persecution borne for Christ's sake is glorious, and illness is not humiliating, while nothing is so calculated as temptation of this kind to remind man of his own frailty, of his entire dependence on grace, of his need to "bring his body into subjection, lest he become a cast-away" (1 Cor. ix. 27). The word *buffet*, again, is usually used of a blow on the face, and so denotes that which is more shameful than painful. Moreover, nothing else could so suitably be called an angel of Satan; and finally, if this be the true interpretation, the obscurity of the apostle's allusion to it is at once explained.

The fact that this interpretation is rejected by the Protestant commentators is one that has no weight, for the reasons on which they base their opinion show an absolute want of perception of the difference between temptation and sin, or of the distinction between innocence and virtue. The only real objection which has been brought against this view is founded on the words of *vv.* 9, 10, *I will glory in my infirmities*. But this is a continuation of what has been said in *vv.* 5, 6, and does not allude to this one thing in particular; though even in regard to this he might glory not in itself, but because it is an affliction sent by the devil, and because by it the operation of the power of Christ is displayed. So St. James says, "Count it all joy, when you shall fall into divers temptations . . . that you may be perfect and entire"; and again, "Blessed is the man that endureth temptation" (James i. 2, 4, 12).

It seems clear that this last view is by far the most probable, both on account of the authority by which it is supported and of its intrinsic adaptability to the context.

## APPENDIX IV.

### THE "LETTER" AND THE "SPIRIT."

"The letter killeth, but the Spirit quickeneth" (iii. 6).

It is evident that the Spirit gives life to men in the Sacraments of Baptism and of Penance, and supports and strengthens it in the other

Sacraments, which owe their power to the Incarnation and the Passion of our Lord: but it is not so obvious at first sight in what sense the "letter" of the law kills. This must be understood in the sense that the precepts of the law are the occasion of eternal death to those who transgress them; for (1) those things which were not already forbidden by the law of nature, would not have been sinful, if not prohibited by the law of Moses; and (2) in respect of what the law of nature already forbade the sin is greater when the command infringed is made more explicit. Thus the precepts of the law give the knowledge of sin without imparting grace to resist it.

It was not therefore the giving of the law, but the sin of those who transgressed it, which was the *cause* of death. But if the law had been given by itself as God's sole gift to men, the result might indeed have been an increase of sin, and the ruin of more souls. It never was, however, and could not be the purpose of God that the law should be a complete or final revelation. And for this reason he made known to the Israelites in prophecy His purpose of their Redemption and that of all mankind, even before the law was given, in order that they might be encouraged to hope for Redemption: and all those who were saved before the coming of our Lord, were saved by the power of the grace brought into the world by Him. Among other means, however, which God chose, to prepare mankind for His coming among them to justify and save them, was the gift of the law of Moses to the children of Israel. This law served in its precepts to keep men from sin by fear; and still more to increase their sense of sin, so as to lead them to humility and penance; and in its ceremonies it symbolized and prepared the minds of men for the great mysteries of the New Dispensation, by which life was given to the world. It was, as St. Paul says (Gal. iii. 24, 25), like the servant whose duty was to take children to the school of which our Lord is the teacher. Those who had the privilege of living under the law before the coming of Christ were therefore under a special responsibility inasmuch as they were under the guidance not merely of the law of nature, but also of a special (although partial) revelation. In the same way, but in a higher degree, those who have heard the Gospel, and either rejected it in bad faith, or accepting it do not lead lives becoming Catholics, will receive greater punishment than those who do not know the truth (cf. Luke ii. 34: John xv. 22).

Besides this, at the time at which St. Paul was writing, the law of Moses was especially liable to be an occasion of death to those who still trusted to serve God by its ceremonial observances, which were now superseded by the realities of the New Testament, which they had prefigured. And this was an error into which the Corinthians were in danger of being led by their false teachers.

This and similar sayings of St. Paul have received various erroneous interpretations from heretics at different times. Origen, and the mystics who followed him, supposed that this verse meant that all Scripture was meant to be understood, not in a literal, but in a mystical sense, and that the latter alone was profitable to Christians. The Anabaptists, at the time of the Reformation, made use of the same passage to excuse themselves from all obedience to the moral law. Finally, some modern Rationalists claim from this verse the support of St. Paul in their desire to understand the Commandments, and other passages of Scripture, not in their literal sense, but in some other sense which they suppose to be the spirit of the passage.

www.ingramcontent.com/pod-product-compliance
Lightning Source LLC
Chambersburg PA
CBHW020137170426
**43199CB00010B/775**